How to Win at Online
Gambling

Senior Executive Editor: Roland Hall
Art Direction: Darren Jordan
Design: Sailesh Patel
Picture Research: Tom Wright
Production: Claire Hayward

ISBN 1 84442 453 7

General Editor's Acknowlegements

Thanks to the contributing authors who devoted their time and efforts to making this book happen. Your expertise is invaluable. Thanks also to Emily for enduring many painful days as an innocent bystander to the authoring process. You're the best.

The Publishers would like to thank the following sources for their kind permission to reproduce the pictures in this book. The page numbers for each of the photographs are listed below, giving the page on which they appear in the book and any location indicator (t-top, b-bottom).

6–7. Corbis/Bill Ross; 28–29. Corbis/Richard Cummins; 54/55. Getty Images/Frazer Harrison; 66–67. Corbis/ Tim Taddler/Newsport; 85. Empics/Batchelo Barry Batchelor/PA (t), Getty Images/New Press (b); 86. Getty Images/Andy Lyons; 98. Corbis/Bob Rowan/Progressive Image; 130. Getty Images/Paul Gilham.
www.PlusLotto.com, www.GoldenPalace.com, www.DrHo888.com, www.CasinoCity.com, www.IGCouncil.org, www.eCOGRA.com, www.OnlineCasinoNews.com, www.CasinoMeister.com, www.WinnerOnline.com, www.Gambling.com, www.GoneGambling.com, www.AwesomeJackpots.com, www.GamblingOnlineMagazine.com, www. freeslots.com, www.InterCasino.com, www.Blackjackinfo.com, www.bjmath.com, www.GameMasterOnline.com,

Disclaimer

Printed in Singapore

www.Blackjack-School.com, www.NewYorkCasino.com, www.ZamZone.com, www.conjelco.com, www.Jazbo.com, www.SlotCharts.com, www.PacificPoker.com, www.888.com, www.Bodog.com, www.Betfair.com, www.WhichBingo.com, www.Bingo.com, www.FunBingo.com, www.OnlineBingo.net, www.CMoftheYear.com, www.PlanetLotto.com, www.LottoLuck.com, www.Globelot.com, www.MahjongClub.com, www.SkillArcade.com, www.SkillJam.com, www.WorldWinner.com, www.MiniClip.com, www.MidasPlayer.com, www.Disoft.tv, Sky Active, www.Ladbrokes.co.uk, wap.WillHill.com, www.GoldenPalaceMobile.com, wap.Ladbrokes.com, wap.PaddyPower.com, www.BetWWTS.com, www.BetandWinn.com, www.PokerRoom.com, wap.RacingPost.com
Every effort has been made to acknowledge correctly and contact the source and/copyright holder of each picture, and Carlton Books Limited apologizes for any unintentional errors or omissions, which will be corrected in further editions of this book.

How to Win at Online Gambling

General Editor: Mark Balestra

CARLTON
BOOKS

CONTENTS

INTRODUCTION

Gambling has long been popular, but it is only recently, with the advent of affordable home computing, that so many people have had such easy access.

INTRODUCTION

The digital age has forever changed commerce, entertainment, and the consumer experience. The world is literally at our fingertips, and it all happened in a matter of five or ten years.

Our computers, cell phones, and televisions are so much more than most of us could have ever imaged. They are our libraries, our banks, our stores, our juke boxes, our newspapers, our game consoles, our stock brokers, our phone books… and yes, our casinos, our sports books, our lottery terminals, and our bingo halls.

So among the many technological advancements of the digital age, you can now fit a poker table, a slot machine, a race track and much more on your desktop—even in your pocket. Welcome to the age of Internet gambling.

How Did It Come About?

Ten years ago the offshore betting industry was beginning to find its stride. Betting over the phone with sports books operating on tropical islands had become an attractive option for punters living in places nowhere near regulated sports betting facilities. Even those with access to terrestrial sports books or corner betting shops were finding that it was easier to phone in bets and that the offshore books sometimes offered better prices.

Around the same time, businesses in all industries

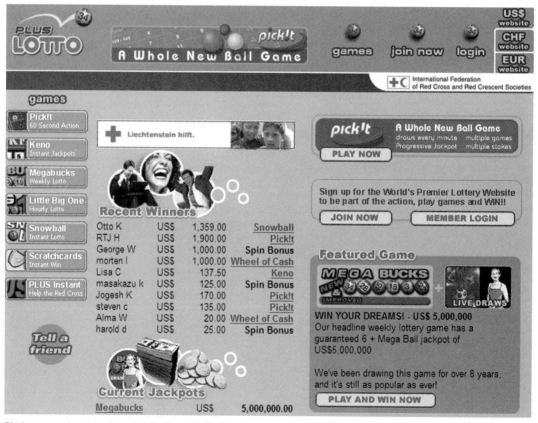

Pluslotto.com played a major role in leading lotteries into the twenty-first century.

were discovering the Internet as a new means of selling their products, and offshore bookies saw the light. Whereas they previously took bets over the phone, they found that they could enhance their services by bringing them online. Offshore businesses like Sports International, Intertops, and WWTS set up Web sites where customers could view odds from menus and place bets via online forms.

Encryption technology enabled the transfer of funds and information in a secure environment in which bettors could monitor their funds, track their bets and view their transaction records. What's more, the services were automated so all of these things could occur 24/7 without human interaction.

The online betting experience has improved immensely since the first Internet sports books popped up in 1995. Encryption technology has gotten better; the Web sites are quicker, more powerful and easier to navigate; bettors have more payment options and quicker access to their winnings; and First World countries have established stringent regulatory standards for sports book operators.

The concept of using the Internet as a point of sale certainly wasn't limited to sports betting. Around the same time the first online sports books were emerging in the Caribbean, a company called Plus Lotto established what is believed to be the first Internet-based lottery, and numerous other businesses—from private companies to lottery agents to state-run lotteries—have followed. Not only does the Internet enable people to purchase lottery tickets remotely, lotteries have added sound and animation to scratch games and the like.

Not long after sports books and lotteries found their way to the Internet, companies began to offer race betting online as well. Internet-based race books and sports books are similar in a lot of ways, although race betting services typically offer pari-mutuel (pool) betting. Services offering betting on horseracing were also among the first to merge traditional (land-based) forms of betting with interactive platforms. For example, betting pools fed by wagering at tracks and off-track betting parlors are now accessible via the Internet and wireless platforms. Another innovation taken advantage of by online race books is streaming media, which has enabled Internet customers to not only place

bets using their computers, but also watch live streamed video footage of the races on which they're betting.

Gambling truly entered the digital age through the advent of games that are actually played on the computer. Players got a taste of computerized gambling via instant lotteries, but the ultimate breakthrough was the arrival of online casinos in 1996. These sites brought games that you would find at land-based casinos (blackjack, video poker, baccarat, etc.) to the computer screens of eager gamblers all over the world.

The flood gates opened in the late nineties, and today any type of gambling found offline can be found online in numerous languages, across multiple platforms, and at all stakes. The Internet has even led to the advent of new forms of betting—most notably betting exchanges, for which an entire chapter of this book is dedicated. And of course there's the latest craze, Internet poker, also covered in this book.

To better understand how Internet gambling grew into such a popular form of entertainment, consider the following factors that have come into play:

IMPROVING TECHNOLOGY – Personal computers are faster, have more disk space, and are therefore more capable of running complex applications. Further, encryption technology has improved, paving the way for the secure transfer of information, particularly banking details. A final prong is the increased availability of broadband, which has enabled gambling sites to offer enhanced versions of their products to wide audiences.

INCREASED AWARENESS – The longer Internet gambling is available and the more the industry expands, the more people are aware that they exist and the more familiar and comfortable they become with online gambling services.

BRAND RECOGNITION – Also raising the level of comfort is the ever increasing presence of large companies with well recognized brands in the Internet gambling business. The idea of giving your money and banking details to an unknown business operating in an offshore tax haven can be a little unsettling, and the arrival of well known reputable gaming and entertainment companies like Ladbrokes, Virgin Group and Playboy has made Internet gambling more appealing to the casual bettor.

STRINGENT REGULATIONS – Numerous governments

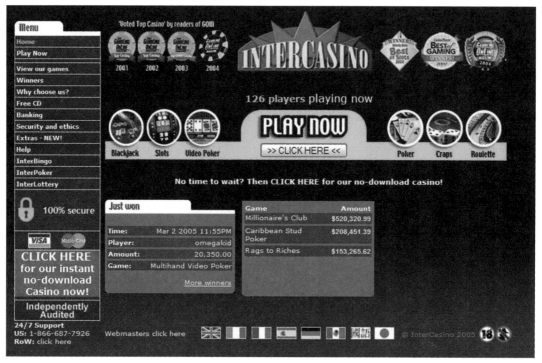

InterCasino was one of the world's first real-money Internet casinos and continues to be an industry leader today.

have answered the popular comparison of the Internet (particularly Internet gambling) and e-commerce to the days of the unlawful "Wild West" by implementing strict controls and regulations for Internet gambling. Cautious online gamblers have some peace of mind, thanks to mandatory software testing, background checks, audits and other procedures carried out by regulatory bodies.

INCREASED INTERNET ACCESS – Simply put, increased access to the Internet from all over the world means increased access to Internet gambling services. And naturally, the growing consumer demand has led to more options for online gamblers. (More than 2,000 sites on the Internet offer real-money gambling services today.)

TRUST IN E-COMMERCE – Consumer apprehension when it comes to making purchases over the Internet has steadily dissipated over the years. People have grown comfortable spending money online and are not as worried about sharing credit card information and

banking details with online merchants. This applies to all e-commerce-related activity, including online gambling.

THE LOVE OF GAMBLING – People all over the world love to gamble, and this is the No. 1 reason Internet gambling has grown into the massive business that it is today. Those who don't have easy access to land-based gambling facilities now have the option to gamble remotely using a personal computer or handheld device. Even those who are close to casinos, race tracks and/or lottery retailers are taking advantage of the convenience of gambling in the comfort of their homes.

Where Are We Now?

Internet gambling has exploded into one of the world's most popular forms of online entertainment. After years of existing in the shadows, it has made the transition into the mainstream, and it is now a $10-billion-a-year industry run by large private and public corporations and regulated by First World governments. Major bricks-and-mortar gambling operations have expanded to offer their products over the Internet, while well known entertainment brands have added Internet gambling to their offerings. And all of them are expanding to alternative interactive platforms like cell phones and interactive television.

Players at land-based facilities are increasingly taking to online gambling as the barriers continue to fall. Internet gamers are finding their way to gambling sites, where they play for money. Fans of televised poker tournaments are trying their luck at the online game, hoping they'll become the next Chris Moneymaker or Greg Raymer (winners of the 2003 and 2004 World Series of Poker no-limit Texas Hold'em tournaments, respectively—both of whom qualified for the event via Internet-based satellite tournaments).

Every type of gambling available in the terrestrial world can be found online, and after years of being perceived as a shady activity, Internet gambling is finally gaining worldwide acceptance as a legitimate form of entertainment.

Your Guide

Now you know the whole story (at least the short version). That brings us to this book, which I hope will serve as a valuable guide for your Internet gambling experience. But before getting into what this book will do for you, let's first make it clear what it does not and will not do:

- ⊛ This book will not make you rich. Neither I nor any of the authors contributing to this book can or will offer advice that guarantees a profitable gambling experience. When you gamble, you risk losing money—lots of it if you're not careful and/or responsible. There is one very important factor that you must never forget: most forms of gambling have a house edge. So coming into the experience, you should know that the odds are stacked against you. That's why they call it "gambling."
- ⊛ This book does not teach you magic. If I had a dime for every guaranteed winning system out there, I could take out each and every reader of this book for a free meal and perhaps have enough cash left over

The Broadband Revolution

All Internet activity entails the movement of data from your computer to a host computer and back. The more media-rich the content is, the larger the files and the more data that must be passed from computer to computer. One of the early hurdles for online gambling was the scarcity of fast Internet connections. In the late '90s, most home users had dial-up connections, meaning that online gambling sites had to make sure their software applications were small enough to download in a reasonable amount of time. The compromise meant that the games weren't as impressive as they could have been, but this began to change around the turn of the decade. Many consumers now have broadband connections, and this has enabled the sites to offer improved products. The graphics are more impressive, the sounds are crisper and the software suites feature more games. Multiplayer games like poker are now accessible to a much larger audience, and many sites are now enabling customers to view the action via streaming audio and video. The broadband revolution has left it's mark on the Internet gambling world, as the quality of the products has improved tremendously over the last five years.

to cover everyone's cab fares home.
- ⊛ Nowhere does this book offer any guaranteed systems for making yourself rich beyond belief gambling on the Internet. In fact, anyone who claims to have a guaranteed system is either trying to deceive you or living in a fantasy world.
- ⊛ This book does not show you how to cheat. It

doesn't show you how to hack online gambling sites, it doesn't show you how to defraud online gambling sites, and it doesn't show you how to unfairly take advantage of other gamblers on the Internet.

- ◉ This book does not recommend specific places to gamble online. The authors and publisher of this book do not endorse or recommend any of the online gambling sites mentioned throughout the book. References made to specific sites are made for the sake of creating examples for the reader.
- ◉ This book does not provide legal guidance. The authors and publisher do not advise as to whether

Internet gambling is legal where you live. The book is intended only for readers located in jurisdictions where it is legal to gambling online.

Now that we've gotten that out of the way, we can move on to the true goals and purposes of this publication.

AN EDUCATIONAL TOOL – It explains what online gambling is, what's available, and how to avoid some pitfalls.

A STRATEGY GUIDE – It should help your chances of winning by teaching basic strategies and tips.

Computerized games aren't exclusive to Internet casinos. The functionality—and even the look and feel—of online video poker machines, for example, is pretty much the same as that of the machines located on casino floors. The only fundamental difference is that computers housing online video poker are accessed remotely (e.g. via the Internet), whereas the computers housing terrestrial video poker are not.

Online and offline gambling converge at DrHO888.com, where gamblers participate in live games that are broadcast via a video feed. Dr Stanley Ho "the King of Macau Gambling" welcomes you with his offer of many types of gambling experiences.

A REFERENCE – It's a guide to which you can refer regularly after you've begun online gambling.

The Basics

Online gambling seems to intertwine the worlds of fantasy and reality. It's real money, but a digital medium. It involves real people who are often represented by on-screen avatars. The games are real, but only as pixels on a screen, not as dice that can be rolled or cards that can be shuffled and dealt. So when you're gambling online, is it virtual betting or is the computer used for betting on a real event? It can be both, and in

this sense, online gambling can be grouped into two categories:

The computer determines the outcome of the bet. In this case, not only is the computer a channel through which parties transfer funds and information to and from one another, but it literally determines the outcomes of every bet made. For example, when you play blackjack at an online casino (at least in most cases), there are no real cards being shuffled and dealt. Instead, the game play is simulated by computer software, and at the heart of every application is a random number generator. Without getting too technical, a random number

Simulated Racing

Horseracing as we've come to know it in a traditional sense, it seems, would fall into the second category of online gambling (the computer plays no role in determining the outcome of the bet), but this isn't always the case. A number of Web sites offer simulated racing, in which you wager on virtual horses running virtual races at virtual tracks. The gambler places bets in the same manner he would if he was betting on an actual race, but the races and their outcomes are entirely computer-generated.

generator is the part of the software that assures the "events" taking place are truly random. Gambling software applications are constructed to simulate play exactly as it would occur with a real deck of cards, real dice or a real roulette wheel. The random number generator is the engine that assures that the simulation is fair and accurate. The same technology is resident in gaming machines (video poker, slots, lottery terminals, etc.) found at terrestrial facilities. On the Internet, games like keno, bingo, instant lotteries, casino table games, slots and video poker typically use random number generators. Even when you're playing alongside—and sometimes when you're playing head-to-head—with other players (table poker, bingo, multiplayer casino games, etc.), the outcome is often determined by a computer.

The computer plays no role in determining the outcome of the bet. In this case, computers facilitate gambling, but the outcomes are determined by events completely independent of online activity. The best example of this is betting on a race or sporting event. You can use your computer to place a bet on such events, but the winners and losers are determined on the track or in the field of play rather than by a computer program. Also included in this category are online casinos in which the cards are dealt and the dice are

rolled at bricks-and-mortar casinos and the players participate by placing bets online and watching the events unfold via live video feeds.

The Bets

When you place a wager at an Internet gambling site, where is your money going and against whom are you betting? The games, cards, chips, dice and tables are all virtual, and everything is happening in the digital domain, but it's real money, and somewhere there are real people accepting it. With this mixture of real and virtual components, it's easy to lose sight of what's actually taking place. There are numerous types of bets, but for the sake of keeping things simple, there are three basic categories (for both online and offline gambling):

Vs. the House—As the term "against the house" implies, this is when the gambler is betting that an event will occur and the house is betting that it won't. Three outcomes are possible: The house wins, the gambler wins or it's a push (a tie). When you play blackjack, for example, you are betting that your hand will beat the dealer's hand, and the casino is betting that the dealer's hand will win. There might be other people participating, but you're not betting against them; each of you is betting individually against the house. Most casino games fall into this category. The same concept applies to sports books. That is, when you place a bet, there has to be someone taking the other side of the bet, and in the case of traditional sports books, it's the house.

Head-to-Head—In some cases, individual gamblers bet against each other rather than against the house. The house facilitates the betting, but does not win or lose any money. The only money made by the house is a commission on winning bets. Poker is a prime example of this model. The dealer distributes the cards and handles the money, but never wins or loses. A second example is betting exchanges, a relatively new phenomenon borne out of the Internet gambling age. Betting exchanges are similar to sports books on the surface. Individuals place bets from a menu of odds. But where they differ is that the other side of every bet is taken by another better and not the bookmakers. This model allows the gambler to determine the odds. Of course, whether they get any action on those odds depends on whether there's a willing party to take the other side of the bet. Incidentally, for those who believe that buying and selling on the stock market is just another form of gambling, stock exchanges fit neatly into this category as well. Betting exchanges and stock exchanges actually function quite similarly.

Pari-mutuel—French for "to wager amongst ourselves," pari-mutuel betting kind of falls into both of the above categories. You're betting that an event will occur and the house is betting that it won't, but at the end of the day, winnings are divvied up in such a way that the house only takes a commission, and ultimately, the money leaving the hands of the losing bettors ends up in the hands of winning bettors. How much you win depends on how many people placed winning bets and, therefore, take a share of the winnings.

The Media

The proliferation of interactive gambling has spanned numerous platforms. This book focuses mostly on Internet gambling, however, the World Wide Web is only the beginning. It is also possible to communicate—and gamble—across closed, private networks called "intranets." The information is passed back and forth in the same way it is on the Internet, but unlike the Internet, intranets are closed-loop networks that are only open to subscribers.

Then there's the wireless Internet. While Internet gambling gave us the freedom to gamble from any location with an Internet connection, mobile gambling (via cell phones, PDAs, etc.), enabled us to bet on the go. As was the case with Internet gambling, mobile gambling has gotten more popular as the number of consumers with capable devices has increased. It started in a text-based environment through which gamblers could purchase lottery tickets and place bets on sporting or racing events. Now, thanks to the latest generation of cell phone technology, you can play animated games on your handheld.

A third, increasingly popular platform for gambling is interactive television. While watching a sporting event on TV, subscribers of iTV services can launch a betting menu on the screen and place wagers using the remote control.

Other interactive channels feature casino-style games. It's a very popular way to gamble, but the distribution is limited. With the exception of the United Kingdom and Ireland, widespread usage of fully functional interactive television services just doesn't exist.

In a nutshell, where there is access to the Internet, there is gambling. While this book concentrates on the three platforms discussed herein, other forms of Interactive gambling—such as kiosks, in-flight gambling and wireless handheld devices designed for usage at casino properties—are attractive options for the high-tech gambler. And who knows what's on the horizon.

The 'Technical' Stuff

That brings us to the nuts and bolts. Fortunately, being a computer whiz isn't a prerequisite for gambling online, but it doesn't hurt to have a basic understanding of what's happening when you place a bet over the Internet.

Online gambling, by its most abstract definition, is simply the transfer of information from one computer to another. The evolution of the online sports book—as discussed in this chapter—is the perfect example: The computer basically replaced the telephone as the device through which the information is passed. Digital bits replaced analog voices.

The transfer gets a little more complex when it comes to playing games online (casino games, bingo, etc.), but the principle remains the same. As is the case with anything you do on the Internet, most of the activity occurs on the host computer. This is the Web site operator's computer, and it can be located anywhere in the world, as long as it's connected to the Internet. When you place a bet on a sporting event, that information is stored on the host computer. When you play an animated casino game, you're using your computer to view activity occurring on the host's computer. Some gambling sites require customers to download and install special software, in which case the graphics, sounds, and animations are generated by the user's computer. But even with these sites, the important processes (namely the random number generation) are happening on the host computer.

FREQUENTLY ASKED QUESTIONS

Where do I start?

You've already taken the first step: opening this book. Of course, there are other resources out there (most are available online; some are discussed in this book), but the general idea here is that your first objective is to educate yourself. Internet gambling can be an enjoyable (and lucrative!) activity; however, it can be equally disastrous if you don't take the steps to assure yourself a safe, entertaining experience. This book will hopefully provide a roadmap for doing just that.

What do I need to gamble online?

Again, the most important element is knowledge, which is why you're reading this book. In terms of materials, you need a computer with access to the Internet. If your computer is capable of surfing the Internet, you're equipped to gamble online. Some sites require the user to have special plug-ins or to download software applications (all of which are easy to install), but if your computer was purchased within the last five years, you probably have the minimum system requirements necessary. Naturally, your experience—as it would be with any activity involving computer entertainment—is enhanced by having a faster processor, a faster Internet connection and more available hard-drive space. The third and thing you need is funds. (See "How do I deposit and withdraw money?") Also note that there are other means of gambling remotely (such as via interactive television or mobile devices), which are discussed in this book.

Is online gambling safe?

If you follow the tips given in Chapter 1 of this book, then gambling on the Internet is virtually as safe as gambling at a traditional casino, track or betting shop. The same risks that exist with all forms of Internet entertainment—particularly those that involve the transfer of money—exist in online gambling. Anyone who uses the Internet should be aware of that there are susceptible to viruses, invasion of privacy, identity theft and fraud, but these risks are greatly minimized by doing research and understanding how to recognize the red flags. While there are many online gambling sites that operate under little or no regulatory control, there are also many that are government licensed and required to meet high standards that assure player protection.

Where do I find online gambling sites?

Online gambling sites are located on the World Wide Web and are accessible through common Web browsers such as Internet Explorer and Netscape. Links to online gambling sites can be found via search engines, gambling portals and other sites with gambling-related information. These access points are discussed in Chapter 1. Then, of course, if you're an avid Web surfer you probably already know that gambling sites will find you, as there's never a shortage of banner ads, pop-up windows, and email campaigns for online casinos, sports books and other sites where you can gamble with real money.

What types of gambling can be done online?

Everything. Casino games, bingo, sports betting, racing, poker, lotteries... You name it. If it's done offline, it's done online. While it's impossible to recreate the experience of being at a casino, a racetrack or a card room, the gambling that's done at these brick-and-mortar facilities also takes place over the Internet. There are even some types of gambling—such betting exchanges and poker—that many people would argue are more suited for the Internet.

Who's operating the sites?

Yes, there are living, breathing people on the other side of the connection, and many of them are highly regarded in the business and entertainment communities. It's easy to assume that Internet gambling sites are all operated by unsavory individuals in banana republics and/or linked to organized crime, but that's a bit of a misconception. In fact, many online gambling operators are well known, respected, and trusted companies. Some are well established gambling brands such as Ladbrokes and William Hill. Others are entertainment companies like Virgin Group and Playboy. Then there are operators like Sportingbet and Casino-On-Net—businesses that built themselves exclusively as online gambling brands

Portals such as CasinoCity.com provide links to hundreds of online gambling sites.

but have nevertheless achieved a high level of respect among the mainstream gambling public. And of course there are the unknown quantities—operators whom most gamblers know littl or nothing about—but even the majority of them run legitimate businesses. But having said that, you should never assume that an online gambling site is fair and honest without doing some research. Steps toward making your online gambling experience as safe as possible are covered in Chapter 1 of this book.

Do I have to play for real money?

No. Plenty of sites offer free games and contests. Many popular sites that feature word games, board games, trivia games and the likes include casino games, bingo and other forms of entertainment typically associated with gambling—all for free. And nearly all sites that offer real-money games have free-play options that enable users to get acquainted with the service.

Do I need special software to gamble online?

It depends. Sports books, lottery draws, race books and other sites that have ongoing play usually allow customers to wager while remaining in their Web browsers. Gaming sites like online casinos, poker rooms and bingo parlors sometimes require special software to create enhanced graphics, sounds and animations. Many casino sites require you to download software; some have in-browser games that require Java or Flash—plug-ins with which most browsers are already equipped. Sites that feature video feeds (race coverage, live casino action, etc.) might require media software, but in all such cases, the software is made available at no charge. In all cases in which special software is necessary, the download and installation process is made as easy as possible.

How do I deposit and withdraw money?

Gambling sites are online merchants, similar to Amazon.com or Netflix or any other Web site where goods or services can be purchased. They offer a variety of payment options, although credit cards and e-cash are the most common. Think of it as purchasing a service. The customer (the gambler) logs onto a secure server and transfers money to the merchant (the online gambling

Associations like eCOGRA and the Interactive Gaming Council require their members to adhere to standards assuring fairness and player protection. Members of these associations display their logos on their sites.

site). This is done by filling out an online form, of which the required fields typically include name, address and phone number, plus the account number for the chosen payment mechanism (credit card, debit, e-cash, etc.). When the form is submitted, the information is sent to the site operator, who deposits them into a playing account.

When you deposit money at an online gambling site, an account is set up and you gamble with that money. The account is accessed by entering a unique user ID and password. For all practical purposes, you've purchase a stack of virtual chips, and if you gamble it away, you can deposit more money into the account using the same technique. Additional transactions (withdrawals and deposits) are made through the cashier page, which is typically accessible through the site's main menu or index page. The main difference between online gambling sites and common online retailers is that gambling sites have to provide a means of withdrawing money. It's the equivalent of cashing in your chips. It's a much more enjoyable process for obvious reasons, but it's also easier because the site's operator already has your banking information. Gambling sites typically give customers several cash-out options, including bank drafts, wire transfers, and the transfer of funds back into an account set up by a third-party processor such as Neteller or Firepay. These processes are discussed in further detail in Chapter 1.

Can I make money gambling online?

Of course you can—and that's one of the exciting things about gambling—but no one should gamble under any circumstances without understanding that you can also lose money. In fact, the odds are stacked against you, so in most cases, you're more likely to lose than win. Therefore, you should never gamble with money you can't afford to lose.

Is online gambling strategy different from offline gambling strategy?

The same strategies used for winning offline games can be used for playing online games, but there are some exceptions. Online poker, for example, requires a different set of skills. In addition to understanding the mathematics of the game, winning poker players learn

What is a secure server?

Never give sensitive information over the Internet (banking account details, etc.) unless the site at which you're submitting the information is located on a secure server. Without getting into the technical details, Web sites on secure servers enable you to enter information without any outside parties being able to see it. The information submitted goes through a process called encryption, which basically means the data is garbled and remains in a non-discernable format until it is off the Internet and therefore safe from outside eyes. The most commonly used form of encryption is Secure Sockets Layer (SSL) technology.

The obvious question, then, is: How do I know it's a secure server? It depends on the browser you're using, but all common browsers use icons to indicate whether a site is secure. Internet Explorer and Firefox display a lock icon in the bottom right corner of the screen when logged on to a secure server. Netscape has a permanent lock icon in the bottom right corner that displays as unlocked on pages that aren't secure and locked on pages that are. Also observe in the address bar that the addresses of Web sites on secure servers start with "https" rather than "http."

how to read their opponents, and many of the "tells" used in the offline game can't be used online. Rather than watching opponents' body language, players have to observe "online tells," such as betting patterns and how long it takes opponents to make decisions in certain situations.

Another type of betting with strategies exclusive to Internet play is betting exchanges (*see* Chapter 5), which for the most part are only available online. Unlike wagering with traditional sports and race books, exchange betting adds the element of observing "the market" and seeking the best prices.

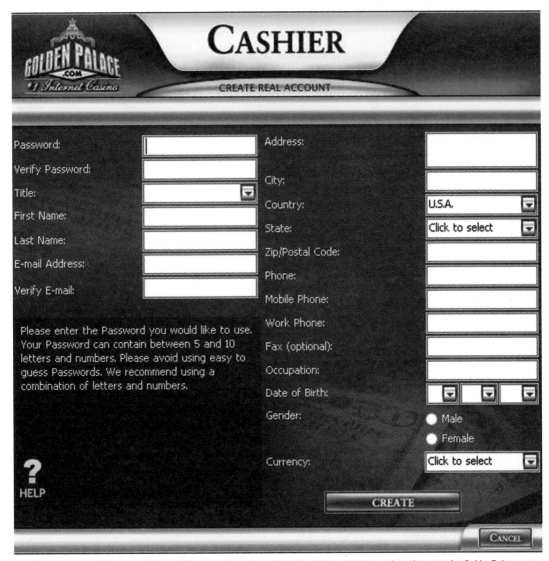

The first step to starting your online gambling experience is registration. Pictured is the registration page for GoldenPalace.com.

Deposits and withdrawals at online gambling sites are made at a virtual cashier, which is accessible from the site's home (index) page, or in the case of separate software applications, from the main menu (a.k.a. "the lobby"). In this example, the cashier is accessed by clicking the link in the top right corner.

Is online gambling addictive?

All forms of gambling can lead to problems if you're unable to control your betting, and the same measures for avoiding problems (outlined in Appendix 3) gambling offline should be taken for online gambling. But Internet gambling presents a new set of dangers as well. First and foremost, playing computer games in general can be an addictive activity in itself, and compounding this danger is that when playing in a virtual environment, it's easy to forget that it's real money being wagered. A second danger of Internet gambling is the fast pace at which the games are played.

When playing online, you don't have to wait for other players to place bets, for cards to be shuffled, for dealers to switch tables, or for chips to be switched out. Internet casino games move at a lightning pace, and it's essential that you keep a close eye on your bankroll. Otherwise your money can vanish in a blink.

Am I playing against real people?

Sometimes. In most cases, casino games, instant lotteries and fixed-odds betting (i.e. traditional sports betting against the house) don't entail playing against other gamblers. Casino games and instant lotteries are generated by software, and no external events affect the outcome. In fixed-odds betting, the computer is basically the bookie's tool for recording your bets and managing the money. For other types of betting—such as table poker, pari-mutuel and betting exchanges—there are other bettors whose activities have a direct or indirect effect on you. They are accessing the gambling sites from remote locations (from virtually all over the world) and taking part in the betting just as you are. In many cases, such as poker, you're betting head-to-head against your opponents and watching their moves in real time as the games unfold on your computer screen. There are also multi-player games (blackjack, craps, etc.) in which you play alongside other players (you can even chat with them over the computer), but your playing with them against the house, rather than playing against them.

What differentiates one online gambling site from another?

Thousands of Web sites offer Internet gambling services, and it's often difficult distinguish one from another. In many cases, they're virtually the same systems operating at unique Web addresses, but there is some variety out there, and the differences are apparent if you look closely.

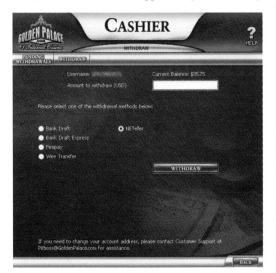

Withdrawing funds should be as easy as specifying the amount and the method and clicking to verify.

On the surface there are unique features like graphics, sounds and animation, as well as the overall theme of the site and how the software performs. More importantly, not all sites offer the same odds and payouts. Some sites make it easier to register and move money in and out of accounts. Other sites offer incentives like special sign-up bonuses, player rewards clubs and refer-a-friend deals. And of course, there are the people behind the site (see "Who's operating the sites?"), and as it is with any business, certain operators have earned a reputation for being fair and honest. The differences are outlined further in Chapter 1, but following are some general questions to ask when differentiating:

- Who operates the site and where is it located?
- How do their odds stack up against those of other sites?
- What kind of software does the site use? Do they require a download or can you play the games in your Web browser?
- Does the site enable you to communicate with other gamblers?
- Is the site certified and regulated? And if so, by whom?
- What methods of payment are available?
- How efficient is the registration process?
- How is the look and feel of the site and/or the games?
- What do they offer in the way of customer service?
- What types of player rewards/incentives are available?

Is Internet gambling legal?

It depends on where the player is located. Every jurisdiction has its own laws, and in many cases, there are no clear laws applying to Internet gambling. In addition to the location of the player, other factors (what type of gambling, who's offering the games, the age of the player, etc.) come into play. The publisher and authors of this book make no assumption as to whether Internet gambling is legal where the reader is located. Nor do they advocate in any way the taking part in games of chance over the Internet if it is not legal to do so. More attention is given to legal issues in Appendix 1.

GETTING STARTED

The first thing you need to know about online gambling is that the most effective regulation in this industry is self-imposed. Certainly governments that license online gaming companies have a strict set of regulations their operators must adhere to, but good online gaming companies impose a code of self-regulation which is vastly more stringent than any imposed by the gaming board.

The Come Out Roll

The reason professionally run online gaming companies run such strict policies of self-governance is that casinos don't need to cheat you to make money. In fact, if you talk to 99% of the I-gaming operators they'll tell you that they want you to win, at least at first. The way ALL casino gambling works, whether online, in Las Vegas or in Monte Carlo, is that the house has a small advantage over the player embedded in the rules of the games. For instance, single numbers in roulette pay 36-1, yet the roulette wheel has 37 numbers (38 in American Roulette). Therefore you can expect to win one in every 37 spins times (assuming that you bet one single number per spin), and you can expect to be paid 36 to 1 (giving the house a 37/36 advantage).

So, the house has its natural advantage that it knows, over time and over a large number of games, will prevail. And while some people will walk away winners and some will walk away losers, the house, in aggregate, will be taking 37/36 of all moneys bet. In other words, by looking at the aggregate number of wagers, and being able to bring enough people to the casino to provide a large enough population for the statistical advantage of the games to prevail, the house will always come out ahead.

On an individual basis, a player can certainly win— and win big—because an individual player won't play enough hands himself for the mathematics to prevail. By only playing a small number of hands (relative to the activity of everybody playing at the casino) the player's "luck" is what statisticians view as variance.

When I say that casino operators want you to win, they truly do, because one winner telling his friends of his luck is worth a thousand banner advertisements. And as we learned from the previous example, more players through the door only help the casino to maintain its 37/36 advantage.

Now that You're in the Know

Now that you know you can trust online gambling sites, you had better learn where to look to find trustworthy ones. If 99% of the casinos out there want you to win, then there is still 1% to watch out for. But knowing who to watch out for and getting ripped off are two very different things. You definitely want to stay away from anyone who may try to rip you off, but with so many good gambling sites, you also have the freedom to choose the A1, 5-star, operators, meaning that you will also want to avoid mediocrity.

Online casino portals are your best bet to identify top operators who will guarantee you a top rate experience. Generally speaking, portals that have either been around the longest, or enjoy the most traffic are the online gambler's best resource. One of the earliest portals is Online Casino News (www.onlinecasinonews.com), and it is loaded with daily new for online gamblers. Its news content is syndicated to hundreds of other Web portals, but you will find it there first. Its advertisers are all handpicked, ensuring visitors a first-rate experience. They also list Top Bonuses, Top casino payouts and highlight some of the biggest jackpots online.

Another top source for gambling sites is Gambling.com (www.Gambling.com), a site that, as you'd guess by the name, focuses on all things internet gambling related. Gambling.com has developed a gambling search engine, which allows users to type in exactly what they are looking for, and the results only pertaining to that query. If you know exactly what you want, you won't find a better site to help you find it.

I-Gaming watchdog Casino Meister (www.CasinoMeister.com) will also get you gambling online in safety. As a watchdog, Casino Meister vets all advertisers before accepting them on the site. But furthermore, Casino Meister is where you go if you ever do have a problem with your online casino. Their

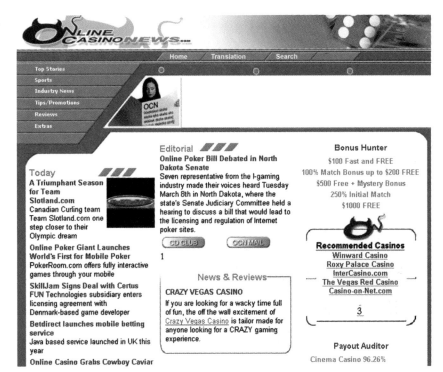

webmasters will listen to player concerns and help resolve issues between players and the casinos.

If Casino Meister is the industry watchdog, then Winner Online (www.WinnerOnline.com) and Gone Gambling (www.GoneGambling.com) are the gossip cats. Here you will hear all the latest from the all sorts of people as both sites run the industry's most prolific message boards. Topics ranging from value bonuses to the color of a dealer's underpants can be forums somewhere on this site, but the real value is that their active message board community will be happy to help with almost any question you can through at them—and they will be speaking from experience.

Slot players shouldn't miss visiting Awesome Jackpots (www.AwesomeJackpots.com), where every major progressive jackpot on the net is displayed in real-time, and if you are serious about slots, then you can do your homework and try and crack when the next jackpot will break using their jackpot history tool. This innovative feature shows you the date and amount of each progressive win from all the major suppliers.

If you're wondering what is happening in the industry, the trade portal iGamingBusiness.com (www.iGamingBusiness.com) will be able to give you a comprehensive behind the scenes look at the online gaming market. Press releases, industry news and industry resources are what this site is about, and you can bet that everybody in the business visit it.

Beyond the Net

Beyond the Internet, gaming enthusiasts can keep tabs on their online casinos through the many quality consumer publications the have emerged since the late 1990. The first and largest of online gaming magazine is *Gambling Online Magazine*. With over a quarter of a million readers, *Gambling Online Magazine* directs online gamblers to the best the net has to offer, with a particular emphasis on reviews of online casinos, sports books and poker rooms. Besides reviews, this bi-monthly publication provides general online gambling advice, to help readers find new sites, bonus offers and new games. Also included in each issue is gambling advice for most popular games, and specific play tips for games at specified casinos. *Gambling Online Magazine* also provides feature interviews with gaming operators, winners and the odd celebrity gambler.

Gamblers in the United Kingdom have *Inside Edge* to guide them through the basics of gambling online. Produced by the people that bring you *Maxim* Magazine, *Inside Edge* is a thick glossy that covers gambling online and off. The focus is of course UK casino, sports, poker and racing; but their is enough online gambling focus to make this a bonafide online gambling publication.

If you're looking for something poker specific, *Bluff Magazine* is one of the newest and most popular gambling

magazines on the rack. Started in late 2004, the magazine quickly grew to more than 200,000 copies, making it America's biggest and most popular poker read. *Bluff*, while not only focused on online poker, covers all areas of poker, without becoming pedantic. *Bluff*'s aim is to get people excited about playing poker, online and off, which explains its popularity.

Bluff's content does of course cover terrestrial poker strategy, but offers special strategic editorial for online poker players, covers online poker tournaments and sends 'Surfer Dude'—their version of a secret shopper—to review unsuspecting poker sites. Their cover stories are usually interviews with celebrities that enjoy the game of poker and have made a name for themselves on the scene, and there certainly are a lot of them. *Bluff* also interviews professional poker players in each issue, and

Gambling Online is a print magazine with an online presence.

has a surprising number of them contributing to the magazine each month.

Another popular poker magazine is *Card Player*. This one is a staple in the serious player's diet. Targeting the pro, semi-pro or extremely serious recreational poker player, card player is known for poker strategy and a comprehensive analysis of the tournament scene. Of course, *Card Player* has also begun to cover online poker, poker's most popular venue. *Card player* is published bi-weekly, so it's ideal if you want what's going on in the world of professional poker without having to wait for it to be aired on television.

All In Magazine is the third poker magazine that you should take notice of. Its format is more like that of *Bluff* than *Card Player*'s format, and it generally has interesting interviews with the pros, tournament coverage and online poker features.

Do It Yourself

If you're a do-it-yourselfer, there are plenty of ways to investigate your potential new online casino without relying on anyone else. You can be as serious a detective as you want, which means you can commit a few hours to investigation or up to several days before you place your first bet.

The first thing a budding online casino Sherlock Homes should do is make sure that the online casino he or she is considering is serious about its customers. Look for the site's customer service options and try them all out. Send them an email asking if they could provide you the details of their licensing authority and, if it's a casino site, the name and phone number of their software supplier. Contact the licensor and ask if the site in question is indeed regulated by the licensing authority and if the site is in good standing. Ask what provisions the licensing authority have made in case the operator takes flight with your deposit and if you want to be doubly sure that your money is safe, ask the licensing authority to provide you with a copy of their online gaming licensing requirements.

For casino gamblers, the next thing to do, if you want a merit badge in investigation, is to phone the casino's software supplier. Once again, you'll want to inquire about the standing of that casino's software license, and you could even cross-reference the contact details of the casino as provided by the software provider with the details you found online. Then ask the provider what other casinos use their software, and if you've heard of some of the names on the list, you can be reasonably assured that your potential casino is a serious going concern.

Some casinos will have built their own software, which is fine, but it will meant that you will not be able to contact a third party for verification of good standing.

Once you've satisfied yourself that the suppliers are happy with the Web site in question, its time to do more digging on your own. Find out more about the owners of the gambling site by visiting a site like www.whois.org, which provides details of the registrant and technical contact for the site. Match those details with the details the operator posts on the gambling web site and make sure that they match. If they don't, get back on the email and ask their customer service team why not.

You should evaluate the site, not only by checking the boxes, but by the speed at which they respond to inquires. You should generally get an answer to any question you may ask within 24 hours Monday-Friday, and some type of response, even if it's not the answer, within a few hours.

Also try out the gaming site's telephone customer service. Almost every gambling service in cyberspace has a telephone support number. Make sure that they are there when you need them. Make sure that they are helpful and that they are courteous. There is so much choice out there that no one needs to settle for anything less than the VIP treatment.

You're not Alone

Even the best investigators sometimes get things wrong, but thanks to the Internet, you have several sources to verify the results of your investigations. Visit message boards and search for topics on the online gaming firm that is in question. You can usually find something helpful if you visit the major message board portals like www.WinnerOnline.com, www.GamblingOnlineMagazine.com, or www.GoneGambling.com.

You would also be wise to check the naughty and nice list at www.CasinoMeister.com if you wanted to find out whether the site you're investigating has a history as a troublemaker.

Your next stops are www.OnlineCasinoNews.com and www.Google.com, where you can run a news search on your potential gaming site. Look for independent editorial on the site in question. There will probably be several articles on the site you are investigating, and its worth it to read them all, from the latest news to the earliest. This builds a timeline as to how the site has developed over the years and as to what the gaming community feels about the site in general. Also look at the press releases distributed from the site being investigated and read between the lines. Press releases can offer tons of information about what partnerships each site has, who its suppliers are, and how many satisfied winners the site produces each month.

Don't fret if you can't find any information about the site in question. Simply ask the members of the gambling message boards their opinion, and you'll find that you get more than an earful. The only caveat on the message boards is that the gaming marketers also traawl the boards waiting to answer questions like yours. If a reply looks too flowery, it may be from the site in question, and if it looks suspiciously negative it may come from their competitor.

Sign Me Up!

If you've never gambled online before, the orientation process might seem a bit intimidating from afar, but signing up and getting started is really quite painless. Following is what you'll need:

- Access to a personal computer with an Internet connection. If you're using a computer that's five years old or newer, then it's almost a sure thing that you have adequate equipment. The essential ingredient, of course, is access to the Internet.

- Very basic computer skills. If you know how to surf the Internet, then you're pretty much there. All online gambling services accessed through their Web page and all of them walk the user through the registration process. If your Web site of choice requires you to download special software, you need to know how to download and install applications onto your computer, but again, the operators of the site will hold your hand if necessary.

- Money and a means of funding your account. Naturally, it's not gambling if there's no money changing hands. All you need here is knowledge of your banking details. The most common form of payment is credit card, and funding an account is simply a matter of entering the numbers into an online form. If the site has a problem processing your credit card information, you can opt for alternate payment systems, such as NETeller or FirePay. To fund these accounts, you need to know your personal banking account numbers. Of course, you should NEVER offer any of this information unless you're in a secure environment. Most sites also give those who are unable or unwilling to conduct a transaction over the Internet the option of paying via wire transfer or personal check, although the only fallback with these forms of payment is that you have to wait a few days for the transaction to clear.

- An understanding of how to play the games— There are many great sources for learning the rules and strategies for all forms of gambling, and these sources are discussed throughout this book.

Bonus Blindness

Sometimes players are blinded by the bonus offered by the sites they're considering and become blind to the good advice offered above. Whatever you do, don't base your decision on where to gamble based on the bonuses offered. Bonuses are almost always beleaguered with ironclad terms and conditions which make the bonuses a dubious advantage at best. Unfortunately, this is a result of player greed rather than the casino's cunning, as "bonusing" started out as a genuine "gift" from the casino to the player. $25–$100 in bonus money used to flow into the accounts of online gamblers, all in good faith that the player would genuinely play with that bonus at the casino that offered it to them. Before long, scam artists found that they could deposit money at casino and make out with the bonus without really playing. This "bonus abuse" forced the industry to rethink the way they offered bonuses. By that time, however, bonusing was such a big part of I-gaming marketing that no one could afford to drop it completely, and the strict terms and conditions were brought in.

Bonus problems are the player's No. 1 complaint about online gaming. Often legitimate players assume that bonuses come with no strings attached. Don't ever assume that. Read the terms and conditions that encumber the bonus and understand fully going in that the bonus will probably net out to zero once the terms and conditions are met.

You've Earned It

Online gaming sites love to hear that they're doing a good job. If you've gone through all this due diligence, then you should tell them about it. Send a message to customer service and bring a smile to the operator's face. You will almost certainly get a polite response, and the site may even ask to post your compliments on the Internet. If they do, you might earn yourself a small bonus (no strings attached) or preferential treatment the next time you call. It will establish you as a serious player the next time you call or email the site, and it will help you get more out of the site than your typical new player. You may not be elevated to VIP status right away, but you have made a step in the right direction.

Likewise, if you have completed all your homework, then you have a right to complain about things that are misrepresented or disappointing about your new gaming site. Send an email and keep a copy of the paper trail. Online casinos expend around $300 to acquire every new player, and they don't want to lose you once you've registered. Again, almost all requests will receive some kind of response, and generally customer feedback, provided it is polite, will be welcomed. What you don't want to do is act derisory toward the gaming site and make yourself out to be a problem customer. If the gaming site answers your request by changing something on their site or software, you owe them a thank you. Again, honey gets you more than vinegar in the online gaming world.

Once you've been a good player for a few months, you're in there. The operator, after seeing a fair and legitimate playing history, will be willing to bend over backwards to accommodate you. Think of the casinos in Las Vegas: They give you dinner, show tickets, suites, the whole shebang. Online casino do that too, although in a more subtle manor. They're happy to rule in your favor over most misunderstandings, offer additional bonuses to good players, and have even been known to send new PCs and other fantastic gifts to their valued customers.

If you want to play online, but were afraid to try, following these simple steps will ensure a safe and happy future in I-gaming. Most people however will not have the time to investigate every site before they play. If that's the case, be smart about how much you play at a new gaming site. Only deposit as much as you can lose without having a heart attack, and test the site by depositing, playing a small amount, and then deducting funds. If the process is seamless and easy, then make your second deposit with confidence. Gambling online is supposed to be fun, and you can't have fun if you are afraid of the site on which you play. What it all boils down to is reaching a comfort zone where you're never in question whether or not your money is safe. Spend your worries on drawing a card with the dealer showing a 6 against your 12, because that type of worry is a whole bunch more fun.

Bet smart and be lucky!

ONLINE CASINO GAMBLING

Time was when you needed to make a trip to visit a casino. Now you can get all the thrills withouth leaving your desk – you can even play at work!

ONLINE CASINO GAMBLING

Casino gambling found its way to the Internet in 1996 and is still a very popular form of interactive gambling. Virtually every game you find on a casino floor is also found online and that's been the case for years. Further, the regulatory approval process for online casino games is often looser and quicker, so many online casinos can offer unique new games. (Although, before you jump all over these games, do keep in mind that most of them don't offer very good odds.)

For the player, the main discernable difference between online and bricks-and-mortar casinos is convenience. All "tables" and "machines" at online casinos are accessible with the click of the mouse, and you can exit one casino and enter the next without leaving your chair.

The main fundamental difference between online and offline casinos (as discussed in the Introduction of this book) is that games decided by the turning of cards, the spinning of wheels and the rolling of dice at bricks-and-mortar casinos are determined at Internet casinos by software that simulates these activities. The one exception is the live gaming format in which the personal computer serves as an interface between the remote gambler and a live dealer. This is more or less "proxy" gambling via the Internet (which can be a very entertaining experience).

Getting Started

Chapter 1 offers the goodies on how to start your online gambling experience, but just to save you the trouble of flipping a few pages back, following is a brief rundown of the bare essentials. You will need:

- Access to a personal computer with an Internet connection. (In case you were wondering about mobile and interactive TV gambling, those topics are discussed in Chapters 11 and 12.)
- Very basic computer skills (surfing the Internet, downloading and installing files, etc.)
- Money and a means of funding your account (discussed in further detail in Chapter 1).
- An understanding of how to play the games. Some of the basics are covered in this chapter, while games requiring more skill are discussed in Chapter 4.

Software Considerations

Internet casino operators deliver their products using two general types of software: games that reside primarily on the server (the Web site host's computer) and games that reside primarily on the client's computer (the computer of the gambler).

Server Games

Server games are played in your Web browser. You register and fund your account using the casino's Web site and enter the games without ever leaving the browser. The most common platforms use Java and Flash technology.

Where does the gameplay take place?

When talking about "client-based" games, we generally think of all the action taking place on the gambler's computer, but that's not exactly true. In fact, the "important" stuff always takes place on the online casino's computers in a secure environment. The graphics, sounds, and animations are generated by the downloaded and installed software applications, but the random number generator and the transaction processing systems are still housed on the server.

THE ADVANTAGES – You can play immediately, you don't have to install software onto your machine, and you can play from any computer with capable Internet browsing software.

THE DISADVANTAGES – Game play is often a little slower, the graphics, sounds, and animations are often inferior to those of client games, and you have to go through the casino's Web site every time you want to play.

Client Games

Client games are generated by unique software applications. The player downloads these free-standing programs from the casino's Web site and than installs it onto his computer. To enter the casino, the player launches the software by clicking an icon, rather than bringing up the games in a browser through the casino's Web site.

THE ADVANTAGES – The graphics, animations, and sounds are much more robust, and the game play is much quicker. Plus, you can launch the casino application from your desktop without have to go through your Web browser.

THE DISADVANTAGES – Forget about instant gratification. You have to go through the download and installation process prior to beginning play. You often have to download upgrades periodically as well. Further, the software takes up space on your hard drive and you can only play on computers in which the software has been installed.

Additional Considerations

How does one online casino differ from the next? Beyond the vetting process described in Chapter 1 (considerations such as reliability, promptness of payouts, customer service, etc.), it really comes down to user preference. Most online casinos carry the same games, and with few exceptions (discussed in Chapter 4) the same odds. So, as it does at a land-based casino, it comes down to going with what you like. Here are some features and characteristics that might help you along in the decision making process:

THE LOOK AND FEEL OF THE GAMES. There's no science involved here. Just decide for yourself whether you like the virtual environment and the way the games flow. Here's where it's nice to try the games for free.

EASE OF USE. User-friendliness is an important feature. Is the functionality clear and easy to understand?

COMMUNITY. Some people enjoy playing multiplayer games and chatting with other players. A lot of online casinos offer these features, although some of them certainly place more of an emphasis on the community aspect.

MODULAR VS. BUNDLE. Casinos that require players to download software offer different types of packages. Some of them bundle the software into one large download, while others allow you to download the games individually.

AVATARS. In the event that you would like to be someone else, some multiplier casinos allow you to select your screen persona by giving you numerous virtual "characters" from which to choose. The character you select represents you as viewed by other players.

Getting the Most out of Your Play

The online casino business has become very competitive, and that's a great benefit to the player. Casinos are battling for your business and more than willing to throw some incentives your way. Assuming all other things are equal (integrity, customer service, quality of software, etc.) these are differentiating qualities to observe:

PLAYER REWARD PROGRAMS – Most online casinos have player clubs that reward customers for extended play. A typical program offers somewhere in the range of 0.1% cash back on bets placed. That doesn't seem like much, but if you're going to be playing a lot, you might as well sign up. In some cases (as explained in Chapter 4), cash-back rewards can mean the difference between a house edge and a player edge.

BONUSES – This is a concept that's been around for years: Sign up to play at an online casino and the casino gives you "seed" money for good measure. Some will match your deposit (up to a certain point), while others will toss in $50 or $100. You should definitely take advantage of this, but before doing so, read the terms! Casinos have to protect themselves from being burned by players who sign up, take the bonus, play a few hands and cash out with a profit, so they require players to play a certain amount before they can withdraw money.

REFERRAL PROGRAMS – Send a friend! Many online casinos will give you bonus money to gamble with for referring new customers.

BETTER ODDS/PAYOUTS – For the most part, competing online casinos pay out at the same rates, but as discussed in Chapter 4, there are some variations of which to be aware. For example, some casinos offer video poker games with better pay tables than others. (You can get the lowdown on these at www.GameMasterOnline.com, by the way.) Then there are the obvious things casino players look for: favorable blackjack rules, European (as opposed to American) roulette, etc.

PROGRESSIVE GAMES – Like land-based casinos, online casinos offer games (known as "progressives") in which the jackpot grows higher and higher until its won. The most common progressives are for slots and video poker. The larger progressive networks, of course, can be very attractive because more players are pouring money into them

Casino Games

Following is an overview of some of the popular games available at online casinos. It doesn't get into a detailed explanation of the rules for each game, but useful links for

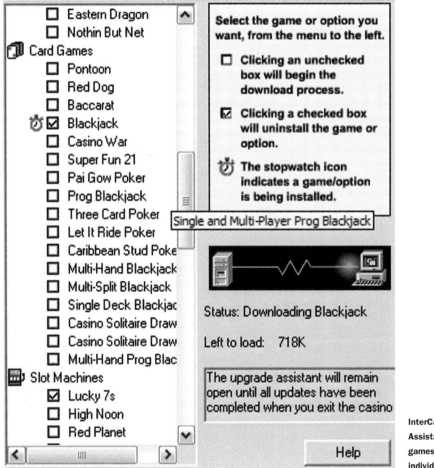

InterCasino.com's Upgrade Assistant enables you to add games to your computer individually.

sites where you can learn the ropes are listed in Appendix IV. As mentioned, what's found online is pretty much what's available at bricks-and-mortar casinos.

Slots

Slots are slots. They can be very entertaining, but they don't require any skill. Simply select the amount of money you want to bet and click the mouse. One thing that's nice about online casinos is that they tend to feature the latest and greatest innovations in slots; some have concepts that are unique to the Internet. The online player has a plethora of slot games to select from: multi-line machines, multi-level machines, progressives, bonus rounds, etc.

HOW THE ONLINE GAME VARIES FROM THE OFFLINE GAME – It pretty much doesn't, other than on the Internet, there's always a machine open, and you can switch from machine to machine or from denomination to denomination on the fly. In both cases, the outcome is determined by a random number generator.

IMPROVING YOUR CHANCES OF WINNING – In terms of strategy, there really is nothing to speak of. The one area in which you can improve your chances is by checking the pay schedules. (Lots of sites post them.) But realistically, if you're all about playing a game that pays, slots are not for you.

Keno

Keno is a numbers game that's a cross between bingo and a lottery. You basically pick numbers at random and

Slots can be played for free at some sites.

hope they come up on the board. For a fuller explanation of the way that the game itself is played, see www.conjelco.com/faq/keno.html.

HOW THE ONLINE GAME VARIES FROM THE OFFLINE GAME – Both Internet keno and land-based keno are determined by computers selecting numbers at random, so the only real difference is that Internet players are accessing the game remotely.

IMPROVING YOUR CHANCES OF WINNING – There is no strategy involved in playing keno. The only way to improve your chances of winning is to look for variations that offer better odds.

Craps

Craps is a dice game in which one person throws a pair

of dice and participants stand around the table and wager on whether certain number combinations will come up. For a walkthrough on the rules, check out: www.winneronline.com/rules/craps.htm.

HOW THE ONLINE GAME VARIES FROM THE OFFLINE GAME – The biggest difference is the excitement level, as craps tables are usually the rowdiest spots in casinos (aside from the sports book during major sporting events). The fundamental difference is that the outcome of online craps is determined by a random number generator rather than the actual rolling of dice. For all practical purposes, the odds are the same, as craps software provides a precise simulation.

IMPROVING YOUR CHANCES OF WINNING – While craps is mostly a game of luck, there are some strategies

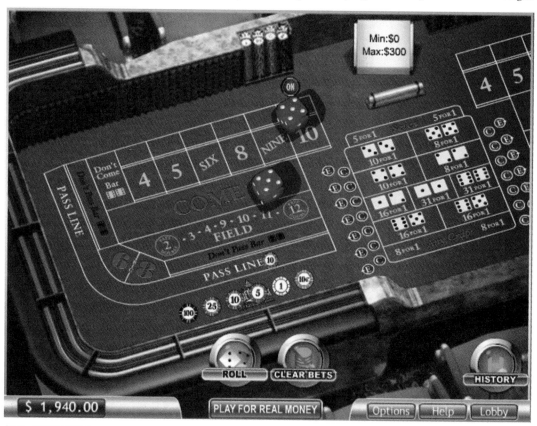

Craps at GoldenPalace.com.

for winning. Those interested should check out the writings of Larry Edell at www.crapshooter.com.

Blackjack

Blackjack is one of the world's most popular casino games. It is a relatively simple card game in which each card has an assigned value and the player tries to achieve the highest value without going over 21. The player wins by having a higher hand then the dealer. He ties (even money) if he has a hand of the same value as the dealer and loses if he goes over 21 or if the dealer's hand has a higher value. For a detailed explanation of how the game is played, you could do worse than pointing your browser at www.blackjackinfo.com/blackjack-rules.php.

HOW THE ONLINE GAME VARIES FROM THE OFFLINE GAME – Online blackjack can be much different than the offline game in that the virtual "dealers" at most online casinos reshuffle after every round. Without being dealt several hands before a reshuffle, blackjack players cannot use card counting strategies. Another major difference is that, similar to craps, the outcome is determined by a computer and not a physical occurrence (in this case, the turning of cards).

IMPROVING YOUR CHANCES OF WINNING – In general, the two keys for the everyday player are 1) playing flawless strategy, and 2) picking a game with favorable rules. Advanced players gain an edge by counting cards and adjusting their bets accordingly. Later in this book we feature a blackjack primer that discusses strategy in further detail.

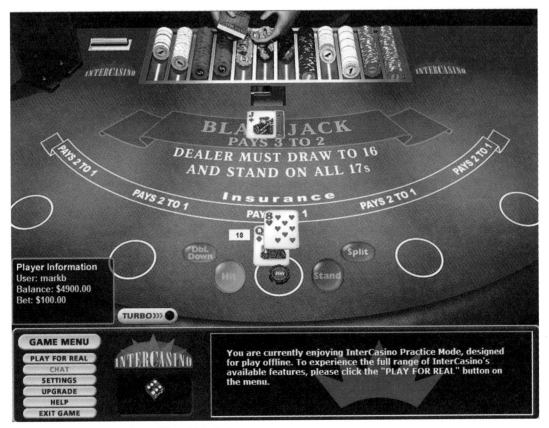

Enjoying the blackjack experience offline at InterCasino.com.

Roulette at GoldenPalace.com.

Roulette

In roulette, a ball is dropped onto a spinning wheel where it bounces around until the wheel stops and then falls into one of many numbered slots on the wheel. Before the wheel is spun, participants wager on where the ball will land. They do so by placing chips on a table, where all the numbers are displayed. A variety of bets cans can be made, including the precise number, a range of numbers, a group of numbers, even/odd and red/black. For an explanation of the rules, visit www.gonegambling.com/rules/rulesroulette.html.

HOW THE ONLINE GAME VARIES FROM THE OFFLINE GAME – Online roulette is no different from offline roulette, except for the computer generated vs. actual occurrence discrepancy. One nice difference in the online gambling experience, though, is that on the Internet, you almost always have the option of playing the French version, which has better odds for the player than the American version.

IMPROVING YOUR CHANCES OF WINNING – Roulette is another game that's determined predominantly by chance. You can place various bets at various odds, ranging from 1:1 to 36:1, but those odds don't change based on the player's skills. The first thing you can do to improve your chances is play French roulette, which has 36 outcomes (a 2.7% house edge), rather than American roulette, which has 37 (a 5.26% house edge). You should also look for a casino that offers the "la partage" rule, which cuts the house edge in French roulette to 1.35%.

Video Poker

Video poker is the single-player version of table poker. Instead of gambling against other players (as they would in table poker) video poker players are gambling against the house (specifically, a computer). The basic rules in terms of building winning hands are the same as those for poker, only in video poker you're trying to achieve certain hands that pay off a specified amounts. For a detailed description of the rules, visit: www.winneronline.com/rules/videopoker.htm

HOW THE ONLINE GAME VARIES FROM THE OFFLINE GAME – Like slots, video poker is entirely generated by a computer, so the main difference between the online and offline games is that the online player is participating from a remote location. There are some other notable differences, which are discussed in Chapter 4.

IMPROVING YOUR CHANCES OF WINNING – The best way to improve your changes of winning is to play games with better pay schedules. And like blackjack, getting the best odds entails playing flawless strategy. The online player, of course, has the advantage of having all kinds of strategy aids at his disposal.

Baccarat

Baccarat is a card game in which two hands are dealt. The "player" and the "banker" each receive two cards. Depending on the value of the hands, each might be dealt a third card as well. All cards are worth face value, except for 10s and face cards, which are worth zero. If the total value of a hand exceeds 9, then the left digit is dropped (e.g. a hand of two 7s is worth 4, not 14). The hand with the highest total value wins. The gambler simply bets on the dealer, on the player, or on a draw. For a detailed description of the rules, see www.casinocity.com/rule/Baccarat.htm

HOW THE ONLINE GAME VARIES FROM THE OFFLINE GAME – Like other card games, the functionality of online baccarat depends on software that simulates game play. The main difference between the online and the offline game is that baccarat at bricks-and-mortar casinos is typically a formal game, while the online game bears a much closer resemblance to the

Gaining an Edge

It is mentioned throughout this book that the house holds an edge in almost all casino games. This is, after all, how casinos make money. But there are always exceptions. Casinos offer loss leaders from time to time in which they offer games with odds in favor of the player. They are few and far between and last for a very short period of time. But in general, there are three casino-style games in which the house edge can be effectively removed on a consistent basis:

- Video Poker – Certain games have pay schedules of better than 100%, but as discussed in detail in Chapter 4, it's not exactly free money. You have to use flawless strategy and you have to be willing to lose a lot of money before the edge pays off.
- Blackjack – Players can beat the house edge in blackjack by using card counting systems, but it's not easy and opportunities to count cards online are scarce. See Chapter 4 for the lowdown.
- Table Poker – There is no house edge in table poker. Instead the house takes a commission from each hand played. The "edge" is gained by building your skills. That's great news, but beware: the competition is tough.

more informal version, mini baccarat.

IMPROVING YOUR CHANCES OF WINNING – The only thing the separates betting on baccarat from betting on a coin toss is that in baccarat, there's a third possible outcome (the draw).

CASINO SCHOOL

Assuming that you've got a firm understanding of the rules for your casino game(s) of choice, it's time to take the next step, which is learning how to make money playing them. Entire books are dedicated to strategy for specific casino games, so it would hardly make sense to cram all the information necessary to be an expert of every casino game into one chapter. This chapter does, however, provide a foundation for learning the proper way to play three casino games: blackjack, table poker, and video poker.

While all casino games are games of chance, there are varying degrees of skill necessary to play each game. On the low end, there are slot games, which require that you know how to press buttons. The three games highlighted in this chapter are on the other end of the spectrum. All are games of chance, but all of them require more skill than most other casino games.

Our resident expert for this chapter is the

The GameMaster's Blackjack School: This in-depth course focuses on Basic Strategy and Card Counting Skills Training. At our web site we have gathered together the entire curriculum, expanded and refined the lessons and added additional resources. If you're looking for the brick and mortar edge this is a great place to start. The lessons are right this way.

GAMEMASTER'S SECRET
NEW **Online Blackjack Tournaments** : The nice thing about Blackjack tournaments is that they allow the "advantage" player an opportunity to use his or her skill in a situation that won't get you tossed from the casino. Now, you can do it all on-line from the comfort of your home. Who's going to toss you out of there? Right this way.

THE LAS VEGAS DEALER:
NEW **MERKLE'S BONER:** There are great baseball stories, the better ones took place before the 1930's. One of the most famous ones is a story I tracked down by a woman called Tillie Merkle-Brown. The first name that stood out was the name Merkle. A die-hard Cubs fan the one only great story of the Chicago Cubs was in 1908. The Cubs last and only World Series thanks to a New York Giant first baseman named Fred Merkle. This is the story of the Merkle's Boner .

FROM THE FELT TOP:
NEW **Happy Birthday Las Vegas:** The Vegas 100's birthday is a little long but funny and interesting. OPENING : It's almost

point for most of my Poker musings, so it's unexplored territory for me. I'm sure my thoughts on this topic aren't original but they might help you win, so check it out.

Lesson 13 - Stealing the Blinds
While we've already covered how to play your hand "on the button", there is a specific opportunity that comes up now and then when you're in that position and you need to know about it. Let me show you how to take advantage of the situation. The pirates are gathering here.

Lesson 12 - Small Blind Math
I'm somewhat fascinated by the Small Blind bet in limit Hold'em poker, which requires you to put up a portion (usually half) of the minimum opening bet and then make a decision about whether to "complete" the bet or just kiss it goodbye. While a previous lesson showed which hands to hold and which hands to fold in a general sense, there are some profits to be made when a lot of players "limp" into the pot, as so often happens in low-limit games. Lesson 12.

Lesson 11 - Playing from Early Position/ Basic Strategy Matrix
In this lesson I'll complete my discussions on pre-flop play of your hand from various positions, plus present my Limit Hold 'em Basic Strategy Matrix, which brings most of the information covered up to this point together in one handy-dandy chart you can refer to as you play. Because you have only a 50-50 chance of improving your starting hand, a good foundation is needed if you want to win.

GameMasterOnline.com offers "classes" for blackjack, poker and video poker as well as the lowdown on which gambling sites give you the most bang for the buck.

GameMaster, whose teachings can be found at www.GameMasterOnline.com. The purpose of the chapter is to scratch the surface with some of the main strategy points for these games and then recommend some specific tips for playing them on the Internet. In these passages, I have condensed lessons from the GameMaster's blackjack, poker, and video poker schools into a crash course of sorts. Should you decide to seek a wealth of knowledge in any or all of these games, www.GameMasterOnline is an excellent place to start.

Blackjack

The key to winning at blackjack is utilizing proper basic strategy. That is, each decision you make on hitting, standing, doubling, or splitting pairs is the correct mathematical play for that hand. Every hand has one—and only one—correct play. To be successful over time, any urge to follow intuition or gut feelings must be ignored. Even when proper strategy leads to a string of losses, you cannot stray.

What, then, is proper strategy? It depends on the rules at the table where you're playing. What are the rules for Hitting? Splitting? Doubling? Is surrendering allowed? Each variation changes the mathematics and, thus, the proper strategy. And if you're counting cards (which we'll talk about in a bit), the number of decks and penetration (how many total cards are dealt before the shoe is reshuffled) come into play when determining the size of your bets.

For those interested in understanding the mathematics behind blackjack strategy, there are some excellent resources out there, such as www.bjmath.com. But if you're in the majority, you're only interested in knowing which plays give you the best chances of wining. The following matrices convey the best strategy for a common version of blackjack. The rules: six decks, dealer stands on soft 17, doubling allowed for any two cards, doubling after splitting allowed, and no surrendering allowed.

Hard Totals

The left column in Figure 1 represents the player's hard totals. The subsequent columns represent the dealer's up card. (In a hard total, the ace is valued 1.)

Fig. 1: HARD TOTALS

	2	3	4	5	6	7	8	9	T	A
17	S	S	S	S	S	S	S	S	S	S
16	S	S	S	S	S	H	H	H	H	H
15	S	S	S	S	S	H	H	H	H	H
14	S	S	S	S	S	H	H	H	H	H
13	S	S	S	S	S	H	H	H	H	H
12	H	H	S	S	S	H	H	H	H	H
11	D	D	D	D	D	D	D	D	D	H
10	D	D	D	D	D	D	D	D	H	H
9	H	D	D	D	D	H	H	H	H	H
8	H	H	H	H	H	H	H	H	H	H

Key:

H = Hit

S = Stand

D = Double; if unable, Hit

Source: www.GameMasterOnline.com

Soft Totals

The left column in Figure 2 represents the player's soft totals. The subsequent columns represent the dealer's up card. (In a soft total, the ace is valued 11.)

Fig. 2: SOFT TOTALS

	2	3	4	5	6	7	8	9	T	A
(A,9)	S	S	S	S	S	S	S	S	S	S
(A,8)	S	S	S	S	S	S	S	S	S	S
(A,7)	S	Ds	Ds	Ds	Ds	S	S	H	H	H
(A,6)	H	D	D	D	D	H	H	H	H	H
(A,5)	H	H	D	D	D	H	H	H	H	H
(A,4)	H	H	D	D	D	H	H	H	H	H
(A,3)	H	H	H	D	D	H	H	H	H	H
(A,2)	H	H	H	D	D	H	H	H	H	H

Key:

H = Hit

S = Stand

D = Double; if unable, Hit

Ds = Double; if unable, Stand

Source: www.GameMasterOnline.com

Splitting Pairs

Figure 3 is a guide for whether pairs should be split. The left column in the matrix below represents the player's hand. The subsequent columns represent the dealer's up card.

Fig. 3: SPLITTING PAIRS

	2	3	4	5	6	7	8	9	T	A
(A,A)	Y	Y	Y	Y	Y	Y	Y	Y	Y	Y
(T,T)	N	N	N	N	N	N	N	N	N	N
(9,9)	Y	Y	Y	Y	Y	N	Y	Y	N	N
(8,8)	Y	Y	Y	Y	Y	Y	Y	Y	Y	Y
(7,7)	Y	Y	Y	Y	Y	Y	N	N	N	N
(6,6)	Y	Y	Y	Y	Y	N	N	N	N	N
(5,5)	N	N	N	N	N	N	N	N	N	N
(4,4)	N	N	N	Y	Y	N	N	N	N	N
(3,3)	Y	Y	Y	Y	Y	Y	N	N	N	N
(2,2)	Y	Y	Y	Y	Y	Y	N	N	N	N

Key:

Y = Yes, split the pair

N = No, don't split the pair

Source: www.GameMasterOnline.com

At a glance, these matrices seem fairly complicated, but from them we can draw the following relatively simple rules (Figure 4):

Basic Strategy Decision Chart

These matrices are examples of a blackjack game using one specific set of rules. For each variation in the rules, the matrices change. Instead of filling this chapter with pages upon pages of blackjack strategy matrices, we recommend visiting www.BlackJackInfo.com. This site features a blackjack strategy engine that spits out strategy charts based on the specific game rules that are entered into a form that's very easy to use.

If you're really serious about programming perfect strategy into the circuits of your brain, the best way to learn is to create flash cards and test yourself over and over. But for the casual player, or the even serious player who's not a big fan of studying flashcards, it is sufficient to have versions of these matrices at your disposal while playing.

Fig. 4: BASIC STRATEGY DECISION CHART

Player's Hand	Decisions
5 thru 8	Always Hit
9	Double 3 thru 6, o/w hit
10	Double 2 thru 9, o/w hit
11	Double 2 thru 10, o/w hit
12	Stand 4 thru 6, o/w Hit
13 thru 16	Stand 2 thru 6, o/w Hit
17 or higher	Always Stand
A,2	Double vs 5&6, o/w Hit
A,3	Double vs 5&6, o/w Hit
A,4	Double vs 4 thru 6, o/w Hit
A,5	Double vs 4 thru 6, o/w Hit
A,6	Double vs 3 thru 6, o/w Hit
A,7	Double 3 thru 6, Stand vs 2,7,8 Hit vs 9,10, A
A,8-A,9	Always Stand
2,2	Split 2 thru 7, o/w Hit
3,3	Split 2 thru 7, o/w Hit
4,4	Split vs 5 & 6, o/w Hit
5,5	Never Split, treat as "10"
6,6	Split 2 thru 6, o/w Hit
7,7	Split 2 thru 7, o/w Hit
8,8	Always split
9,9	Split 2 thru 9 except 7; o/w Stand
10,10	Never Split
A,A	Always Split

Source: www.GameMasterOnline.com

The House Edge

Now that you you've gained a relatively painless means of becoming a blackjack strategy expert, here's the bad news: Even if you play perfect strategy, the unbreakable law of averages dictates that you will lose money over time. Regardless of the rules, the house always maintains an edge (usually in the range of 0.10% to 0.60%), and of course, that edge increases with every time a player fails to play proper strategy. Sorry, but that's the nature of gambling. This is why casinos are extremely profitable businesses, and this is why you should never play with money you can't afford to lose.

But this cloud has a silver lining. Blackjack is unique

in that it is the only casino game in which the house can be beat despite carrying an edge over the players. Professional blackjack players win money by employing card counting systems. There are various techniques for doing so, and the processes can be complicated, but the basic principle of card counting is keeping track of what cards have been dealt to get a better idea of what cards are about to be dealt. While the deck is reshuffled every hand in games like poker, numerous blackjack hands are dealt before the decks are reshuffled. You know that with a freshly shuffled deck, each individual card has a 1 in 52 chance of appearing, but those numbers change as cards are dealt. For example if you turn over 26 cards from a deck and three aces appear, the probability of an ace appearing has gone from 1 in 13 before the first card was turned to 1 in 26 (because know that there's one ace left out of 26 cards.)

Blackjack players use these shifting numbers to their advantage by betting larger amounts of money at points in the game in which they can better assess the likelihood of certain cards being turned. The overall concept is simple, but three factors make counting cards much more challenging: 1) Most blackjack games use multiple decks of cards (typically six), so the mathematics become much more complicated. 2.) The cards are always reshuffled before burning through the entire shoe, limiting the accuracy with which the card counter can predict what's coming next. 3.) Card counters are not welcome at casinos, and even though counters aren't cheating, the casinos reserve the right to give them the boot.

One other thing to keep in mind: Before you can even consider counting cards, you have to learn proper strategy like the back of your hand; it has to become second nature. There's no time consult cheat sheets or flash cards because you are instead concentrating on keeping track of the cards.

As mentioned, there are different methods for counting cards, and entire books are dedicated to these techniques. If you're interested in learning this skill, a good place to start on the Internet is the GameMaster's Blackjack School at www.Blackjack-School.com.

The Online Experience

How do these strategies translate to the online game?

The rules for online blackjack are the same as at bricks-and-mortar casinos, so basic strategy stays the same. There are, of course, nuances (in addition to the obvious physical differences). The online game moves much more quickly than the bricks-and-mortar game, for example, so you have to stay sharp to avoid costly careless errors. And even if you play proper strategy, you have to be willing to absorb larger losses than you'd absorb offline because fast game-play means you can tear through a string of tough-luck hands before you realize what's hit you. One advantage of online blackjack is that you rarely have to wait for a table. It's often hard to find a seat at a land-based casino— particularly if you're looking for a low-stakes game— but unless there's a problem with your computer or Internet connection (or the host site's equipment), there's always a seat waiting for you online.

There is, however, one very distinct downside of Internet blackjack: Opportunities for card counters are very limited. The beauty of counting cards online is that you don't have to worry as much about getting the heave ho. (Counting cards is not illegal, but casinos reserve the right to kick you out if they don't like the way you're playing... and they most certainly will.) But the problem with counting cards online is that nearly all online casinos shuffle the cards after every round.

That said, there are a few exceptions. One of them is Global-Player Casino (www.global-player.com), where the cards for two-, four-, and six-deck blackjack games are dealt anywhere from 35 to 55 percent into the shoe. Another exception is software provider CryptoLogic's casino suite, which features a multi-hand blackjack game that deals several hands into the shoe and is featured at CryptoLogic-powered casinos such as www.InterCasino.com. Another software provider, Playtech, offers a suite of live games in which real cards are dealt by real dealers and the players communicate with dealers over the Internet. As they would at a bricks-and-mortar casino, the live Internet blackjack dealers deal into the shoe rather than reshuffling after every round. The live Playtech games are offered at numerous online casinos, including New York Casino (www.newyorkcasino.com) and Golden Palace Casino (www.goldenpalace.com).

Online Gambling   www.888.com
◉ Blackjack   ○ Slot Machines   Play Now?
○ Roulette   ○ Video Poker   [Yes] [No]

CASINO ON◆NET

THE GAMEMASTE
Blackjac
School

ADVERTISING   CONTACT   BLACKJACK SCHOOL ON DVD/CD

FRONT PAGE   DVD-CD PAGES   OTHER RESOURCES   BLACKJACK SCHOOL ADVISOR

Welcome to The GameMaster's Blackjack School

A brief introduction.

I am very pleased and proud to announce the opening of our newest GameMaster internet presence... **The GameMaster's Blackjack School**. For those who aren't familiar with my "school", **this is a series of 24 written lessons that can teach you how to play a winning game of Blackjack.**

When the state of Missouri legalized casino gaming in 1994, I developed a course of instruction that would show people how to get an edge over the casino Blackjack games. This course, which was taught by me at my home, originally cost $400 and that included all of the training materials, four "classroom" sessions of about 2 hours each, which were spread out over a four-week period and one playing session where I went to a local casino with my graduates in order to assess their skills in the heat of battle, so to speak.

In 1995, I was one of the founders of **Rolling Good Times Online** (rgtonline.com), the Internet's first gambling "E-zine" and that was when I began converting my course into a series of written lessons for presentation as a free, internet-based "school". Those lessons have remained pretty much unchanged over the years and have now been

The GameMaster's Blackjack School on DVD $30

THE CURRENT "GAMEMASTER BLACKJACK SCHOOL" LESSONS:

The Basic Course:
Blackjack School-Lesson 1
Blackjack School-Lesson 2
Blackjack School-Lesson 3
Blackjack School-Lesson 4
Blackjack School-Lesson 5
Blackjack School-Lesson 6
Blackjack School-Lesson 7
Blackjack School-Lesson 8
Blackjack School-Lesson 9
Blackjack School-Lesson 10
Blackjack School-Lesson 11
Blackjack School-Lesson 12
The Advanced Course:
Blackjack School-Lesson 13
Blackjack School-Lesson 14
Blackjack School-Lesson 15

The GameMaster's entire blackjack school can be attended at www.blackjack-school.com. Tuition is free!

Poker

Before delving into the world of online poker, we first must make one very important distinction: We're talking about table poker, not video poker. It's easy to tell the difference between table poker and video poker at a bricks-and-mortar casino. One is an electronic game that's played by dropping coins into a machine and pressing buttons, while the other consists of real people sitting at felt-topped tables playing with real cards. The distinction isn't as easy to make online because both games entail player sitting at a computer playing a game through an electronic interface. But the differences go well beyond the apparent, and the most important distinction is that video poker is a game in which the gambler is playing against the house and in table poker the participants play against each other.

The game we're talking about here is table poker, and

in the last two years it has exploded into what's arguably the most popular form of gambling on the Internet. Table poker comes in even more flavors than blackjack, but in this section, we concentrate on Hold'em, which is by far the world's most popular poker game. We specifically focus on Limit Hold'em, for no other reason than it's much more suited for beginners. And similar to blackjack, and most casino games for that matter, mathematics play a key role the decision making process. Of course, poker is unique in that much of the strategy involves "reading" your opponents, but it is important to not lose sight of the importance of understanding the mathematical aspects of strategy as well. In recognition of this very important element, we have included throughout this passage some basic charts illustrating the math.

Use the following key when interpreting the charts:

Cards valued 2 through 10 are represented by numerals.

- A = Ace
- J = Jack
- Q = Queen
- K = King
- s = any card of the same suit
- o = any card of off-suit
- x = any card

You will also encounter discussion about position play and the various positions at the poker table. (These are explained in Chapter 3.) The following diagram provides a visual of the various table positions:

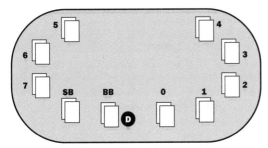

- BB: Big Blind
- SB: Small Blind
- 0: The Button
- 1–2: Late Positions
- 3–5: Middle Positions
- 6–7: Early Positions

Basic Poker Math

Texas Hold 'em players should at all times be aware of their outs. That is, they should know specifically which cards can help their hands and how many of those cards ("outs") remain in the deck. This way, the player knows his chances of improving his hand. Likewise, the player needs to be cognizant of what hands beat his current hand, what hands beat the hand(s) he is hoping for, and the opponents' chances of having those hands.

For starters, Figure 5 (overleaf) shows the probabilities for various hands you might hold after the flop. The probability of success, of course, is based on you seeing two more cards: the turn and the river.

Etiquette is a Piece of Cake

Table poker is offered over the Internet in an automated format, and virtually all Internet poker games make it impossible to break etiquette rules. You couldn't bet out of turn, raise the wrong amount or do anything else considered poor etiquette if you tried. The pot total is always displayed and updated bet-by-bet, the player is anonymous (beyond displaying his or her "handle"), and the games move quickly (at least twice as fast as most bricks-and-mortar poker games).

Rigged?

Internet poker rooms earn their profits by taking a commission from each round, so they are totally disinterested in how well individual players do. None of the money you win comes from the house. Therefore, contrary to the complaints of some who've had bad poker experiences, it's very doubtful (and certainly not logical) that the games would be rigged. The only potential for cheating is on the part of players colluding with one another. Most Internet poker rooms are very thorough about monitoring for collusion and removing suspicious players. It's in the thorough when it comes to keeping things clean.

Fig. 5: FLOP PROBLEM 1

Hand at the Flop	Becomes	At this rate of probability
Two-pair	Full House	17%
4-card Flush	Flush	35%
4-card open-ended Straight	Straight	32%
4-card inside Straight	Straight	17%
Any Pair	3-of-a-kind	9%
Any 3-of-a-kind	4-of-a-kind	4%
Any 3-of-a-kind	Full House	24%

Source: GameMasterOnline.com

Figure 6 shows the probabilities for hands you're more likely to fold:

Fig. 6: FLOP PROBLEM 2

Hand at the Flop	Becomes	At this rate of probability
3-card Flush	Flush	4.1%
3-card Straight (like 5,6,7)	Straight	2.6%
Ace-high	Pair of Aces	12.2%
Ace-high	Trip Aces	0.3%
A-Ko (Aces&Kings)	Two-pair	1.4%

Source: GameMasterOnline.com

If you're interested in the math involved in assembling these charts, then check out the website: www.math.sfu.ca/~alspach/computations.html.

STARTING HANDS – Setting raise and re-raise scenarios aside for the moment, the most important thing to remember is: Play if you have good cards. Fold if you don't. That seems obvious—it's like advising a stock broker buy low and sell high—but you'd be amazed by how many people abandon this very simple strategy. Pocket cards have three possibilities: pair, suited or unsuited. Pairs can be improved in many ways; high pairs often win on their own. Suited cards of different rank can win by turning the hand into a flush, a straight or a straight flush. They can also be improved to two-pair, trips, etc.

Figure 7 is a list of minimum starting hands for Limit Texas Hold'em. The first letter in each cell represents the higher of the two cards. Pairs are not listed because all pairs are playable at one time or other. Keep in mind that this list if for Limit Hold'em. No-Limit Hold'em is a whole other animal.

For help interpreting this chart, let's take a look at the ace column. The first row—"A-xs"—means that if the lower card is of any rank and is suited, the hand is playable. The second row—"A–10"—means that if the other card is not suited, it's only playable if it's a 10 or higher. Therefore an ace-high hand is only playable if it's paired with another ace, a suited card or an unsuited card that's 10 or higher.

Remember—and it can't be stressed enough—just because a hand is playable doesn't mean it should be played in all circumstances. A 10-7s is hardly playable, for example, following three raises. We'll get into betting scenarios in a moment.

POCKET PAIRS – It's always a welcome sight when a two-of-a-kind shows up in your starting hand. We've already established that any set of pocket pairs is potentially playable, but before going all in, let's take a step back and observe the situation. Pocket pairs can be a make-or-break starting hand. They can lead to big hands if the cards on the board provide some help, and sometimes they win pots on their own. But they can also be a road to disaster. Far too often is the beginning poker player drawn into expensive hands because he's

Fig. 7: POKER CHARTS START

A-xs	K-xs	Q-8s	J-7s	10-7s	9-6s	8-5s	7-5s	6-4s	5-4o	4-3s	3-2s
A-10o	K-9o	Q-9o	J-8o	10-8o	9-7o	8-6o	7-6o	6-5o	5-3s	3-2s	

enamored by his starting hand. The flop comes, and he's still only got a pair, but he keeps calling because he's chasing a set or a full house. The turn comes, and still nothing. Now he knows it's not looking good, but he's already invested a lot in the hand and he stays the course because there's no turning back. Suddenly the thought of those two cards that were so pretty to look at when they first came a long have you reaching for the antacids.

To avoid the pocket pair nightmare, a mathematical understanding of the game, once again, goes a long way. First, some pocket pair facts:

- The probability of being dealt any pocket pair is 5.9% (16 to 1).
- The probability of being dealt a specific pocket pair (A-A, 3-3, etc.) is 0.45% (220 to 1).
- The probability of hitting a "set" on the flop (a pocket pair plus a third card of the same rank on the board) is 10.8% (8.26 to 1).
- The probability of hitting quads on the flop, when holding a pocket pair, is 0.25% (399 to 1).
- The probability of hitting a full house on the flop, when holding a pocket pair, is 0.74% (133 to 1).

No set, no bet!

A general rule for playing pocket pairs is that if you hold 9s or lower and don't make a set on the flop, fold.

Figure 8 shows the minimum hands needed to make a play depend on your position at the table. The "button" is the acting dealer, and the following numerals go seat by seat backward from the dealer. The final two seats are the small blind and big blind respectively. The options are to raise, re-raise, call, or fold. It should be noted that this chart is for limit Hold'em under tight circumstances. (In other words, the bets aren't flying left and right.) It is also important to note that to make money, you'll have to loosen your play as the number of players at the table decreases. A hand of 5-5 may not be

all that strong in a game with 10 players, but head-to-head with someone it will often be the winner if it's played aggressively.

Fig. 8: MIN POCKET PAIRS FOR LIMIT HOLD'EM POKER

Position	Reraise/Raise	Call all raises	Call 1 bet only
0 (button)	K-K/10-10	8/8	2/2
1	K-K/10-10	8/8	3/3
2	K-K/10-10	8/8	4/4
3	K-K/J-J	9/9	5/5
4	K-K/J-J	9/9	6/6
5	K-K/J-J	9/9	7/7
6	K-K/Q-Q	10/10	8/8
7 (UTG)	K-K/Q-Q	J-J	9/9

Source: GameMasterOnline.com

The Truth about Low Pairs

Take note: even as a pair, 2s and 3s have very little potential. Call one raise maximum with them and if you don't improve on the flop, get out while you can.

POSITION PLAY—As stated in Chapter 3, how you bet is very heavily influenced by your position at the table. The blinds, for example, have no choice but to ante up, and they're often very soon faced with the decision of whether they want to call a raise to stay in or kiss the ante goodbye. The player on the button, on the other hand, has the luxury of being the last one to act. He can get out of re-raised pots without it costing him a penny, and he can steal the blind if everyone in the early and middle positions folds. Much of Hold'em strategy involves position play. We'll provide a few pointers for playing at each position, but let's first get it all out on the table (pun intended) with the following chart (Figure 9), which shows suggested plays.

Fig. 9: MINIMUM HANDS FOR VARIOUS TABLE POSITIONS

Position	Re-raise/Raise	Call All Raises	Call 1 Raise Only	Call Only ("Limp")
UTG (#7)	A-A, A-Ks, K-K/A-Ko,Q-Q	A-Qs, J-J	A-Js, KQs, 9-9	A-Jo, K-Qo, 8-8
EP (#6)	A-A, A-Ks, K-K/A-Ko,Q-Q	A-Qs, 10-10	A-Js, KQs, 9-9	A-Jo, K-Qo, 8-8
MP (#5)	A-A, A-Ko, K-K/A-Qs, J-J	A-Qo, K-Qs, 9-9	A-Js, K-Js, Q-Js, 8-8	A-10s, K-Jo, Q-Jo, J-10s, 7-7
MP (#4)	A-A, A-Ko, K-K/A-Qs, J-J	A-Qo, K-Qs, 9-9	A-Js, K-Js, Q-Js, 7-7	A-10s, K-Jo, Q-Jo, J-10s, 6-6
MP (#3)	A-A, A-Ko, K-K/A-Qs, J-J	A-Qo, K-Qs, 9-9	A-Js, K-Js, Q-Js, 6-6	A-10s, K-Jo, Q-Jo, J-10s, 5-5
LP (#2)	A-A, A-Ko, K-K/A-Qs, K-Qs, 10-10	A-10s, K-Qo, 8-8	A-5s, A-Jo, K-9s, Q-10s, J-10s	A-10o, K-Jo, Q-Jo, 10-Jo, 10-9s, 4-4
LP (Cutoff - #1)	A-A, A-Ko, K-K/A-Qs, K-Qs, 10-10	A-10s, K-Qo, 8-8	A-5s, A-Jo, K-9s, Q-10s, J-10s	A-10o, K-Jo, Q-Jo, 10-Jo, 10-9s, 3-3
Button (#0)	A-A, A-Ko, K-K/A-Qs, K-Qs, 10-10	A-2s, A-10o, K-2s, K-Qo, Q-8s, Q-Jo, J-10s, 10-8s, 8-8		A-2o, K-8o, Q-9o, J-9o, 10-9o, 9-8o, 8-7o, 7-7, 7-6s, 6-6, 6-5s, 5-5 to 2-2
				Complete Only
Small Blind	A-A, K-K, Q-Q/A-Ko, A-Qs, K-Qs	A-2s, A-Jo, K-2s, K-10o, Q-8s, Q-Jo, J-J, J-7s, 10-10, 10-8s, 9-9, 9-8s, 8-8 to 4,4		A-8o, K-8o, Q-9o, J-8o, 10-9o, 9-8o, 8-7o, 7-6o, 6-5s, 5-4s, 4-3s, 3-3, 2-2
Big Blind	A-A to J-J/A-Ko, A-Qs, K-Qs	A-2s, A-10o, K-2s, K-Jo, Q-2s, Q-Jo, J-2s, J-10o, 10-10, 10-xs, 9-9, 9-xs, 8-8, 8-5s, 7-7, 7-5s, 6-6, 6-4s, 5-5, 5-3s, 4-4, 4-3s, 3-3	A-2o, K-9o, Q-9o, J-8o, 10-8o, 9-7o, 8-7o, 7-6o, 6-5o, 5-4o, 4-3o, 3-2s, 2-2	

Source: GameMasterOnline.com

THE BIG BLIND – No matter how bad your cards are (even the proverbial "worst hand" of 7–2o), you should never fold a big blind hand in an un-raised pot. Lighting does strike at times, and you're already committed the money. The most important decision, then, is deciding whether to call a raise and/or re-raise. It's also important to observe how others fold because you might be able to steal the big blind by raising (provided, of course, that everyone else folds).

THE SMALL BLIND – The small blind requires a lot more thought than the big blind bet because it costs a certain amount of money "complete" the bet, even in an un-raised pot. The decision to fold is often made because the bet has been raised, but there are times when you should fold simply because the cards don't warrant any

further investment. And if you match, what do you do if someone raises from there? When it comes to playing in a loose game from the small blind, you often have to decide whether you're defending your blind from someone who's trying to "steal," someone who's playing a real hand, or someone who's just throwing his money away.

ON THE BUTTON – Occupying the button is the most desirable position in Hold'em; all the other players, except for the blinds, must act before you on the first round of betting, and after the flop, everyone still in the hand has to act before you. This gives you a lot more hands to consider playing.

THE LATE POSITIONS – The late position players, as defined in this text, are the two players acting before the

Advice from the GameMaster:

Betting the small blind isn't as cut-and-dried as betting the big blind because your initial investment is smaller and a lot more depends upon the "texture" of the game. The game you're in may be "loose," for example, in the sense that 50% or more of the players are seeing the flop, even when the bet's been raised. Loose games typically see a lot of pre-flop raises (and calls), which can be a profitable situation for the wise player who plays good hands, whether from the blinds or not.

Limp and Re-Raise

A common betting tactic used for bringing the pot up is limping and re-raising. It's a relatively simple technique: A player "limps" into the pot by calling the big blind and then re-raises any raises when it comes back to him. The reason for this—particularly in a typical limit game—is that upfront raises cause a lot of players to fold, the raiser often wins only the blinds. But by re-raising, the player traps a few players into staying with the hand.

player on the button. The player acting directly in front of the button is in the "cutoff" position. This can be problematic because if the button makes "position raises" in an effort to steal the blinds, you could find yourself betting on a hand that isn't worthwhile. To avoid this, you should play good hands from the late position.

THE MIDDLE POSITIONS – The middle positions, then, are the two or three players acting before the two late

position players (assuming a nine- or ten-player table, respectively) players who act before the two late-position players. The further away from the button you get, the fewer the number of hands that can be played profitably. Because of the possibility of being raised by the late-position players, the minimum starting hands of middle-position players are relatively high.

THE EARLY POSITIONS – The early positions are the first two seats to bet following the blinds. Common sense says that if you raise from the early position, it is likely that you'll be called or re-raised. Therefore, playing from the early positions requires having a strong hand. So, if the average hand played on the button is a J-10 or 8-8, then the average hand under the gun (the first position after the blind) should be A-Q or J-J.

The Online Experience

Unlike blackjack and video poker, online Texas Hold 'em is significantly different from the offline game. The rules are the same and the strategy is the same, but so much of playing successful poker revolves around "reading" your opponents, and there are many more opportunities to pick up on "tells" playing in the flesh. That's probably the biggest disadvantage of the online game for the experienced player. For the novice, perhaps it levels the playing field a bit.

Of course, Internet poker has its advantages as well. For starters, don't think that you can't "read" your opponent just because you can't watch his every move. There are always detectable nuances in your opponents' betting methods, such as their calling, raising and folding tendencies and the amount of time it takes them to act in specific situations. Additionally, the Internet game provides an excellent opportunity to improve your game. Most online poker rooms offer free-play tables, enabling poker novices and Internet novices to get a feel for the games without spending any money. But beware: free-play games are much looser than real-money games, and you'll often find yourself playing hand after hand in which no one seems to be folding (not a very realistic scenario). Another advantage of playing online is you can play with a cheat sheet at your side. There's no reason why you shouldn't know your chances of winning at all times under all circumstances. If you've got it all in your head, then congratulations! If not, use a cheat sheet!

So how do you know where to play online? There's not a huge difference in poker software from site to site, but there are differences in clientele. Some sites, like Poker Stars, have a reputation for bringing in a high caliber of player, while others, like Party Poker, are known to attract a lot more casual (and often less skilled) players. Another thing that varies from site to site is the way tournament are conducted; the total number of chips at the onset and how quickly the blinds increase dictate how the games are played. In staying with the Party Poker/Poker Stars comparison, Party Poker tournaments start with fewer chips, and the blinds increase at a faster pace. The result is a looser game that's a bit more of a crapshoot.

If you're shopping for a place to play, and you want to find the poker room that's right for you, check out the forum www.twoplustwo.com. Here you'll get the lowdown on the Web's most popular poker rooms and plenty of suggestions for which sites are best suited for your game.

Video Poker

The first thing you should know about video poker is that certain versions pay out more generously than others. And the appeal of video poker is that the player can tell a good machine from a bad machine at a glance (unlike a slot machine, where there's no way to tell how well it's going to pay just by looking at it). In video poker, a "good" machine is one that pays back more money in the long run compared with another machine.

Video poker games often pay back more money than what's put in, and this is how video poker differs from the other games discussed in this chapter. We know that there's no house edge with table poker because table poker players are playing against one another rather than against the house. And we know that unless you're an effective card counter, the house always holds an edge in blackjack. (There are exceptions, but these are extremely rare and aren't available for very long.)

Video poker, on the other hand, is the online casino game in which the house—on a consistent basis—doesn't always hold an edge. Casinos don't just give money away, so how do they pull this off? Well, the only way to get an edge on the house is to play perfect

strategy. The house is counting on the majority of video poker players not using perfect strategy and that's a pretty safe bet on their part. This is what makes video poker a great game for both the house and the player. Casinos make loads of money off casual players who are more interested in having fun then playing perfect strategy, while serious players have a nice opportunity to win some bucks if they play the game right.

But before you rush to an online casino with perfect strategy expecting to become a gazillionaire, consider this: The payout numbers are high because of the huge payout of a royal flush, and royal flushes are rare. (For most games, they come roughly once in every 40,000 hands—assuming perfect strategy is employed—but this varies when you bring in jokers, wild cards, etc.) It's true that your expected win rate is good, but you only realize this advantage over the long haul. So if that's the route you want to take, you might want to start by brewing a pot of coffee.

Getting back to the slots comparison, video poker software is not programmed to give a specific return like slots; the return is instead determined by the pay schedule and by how the player deals with that pay schedule. The obvious question, then, is, "How do I know which games pay better?" This leads us to the notations you see regarding video poker machines like 9/6, 10/7, etc. The pay schedule shown on your computer screen is what determines the payout, and the notations are essentially "shorthand" for describing the game.

For example, see Figure 10:

Fig. 10: VP CHART 96-97

Royal Flush	4000	Royal Flush	4000
Straight Flush	250	Straight Flush	250
Four-of-a-Kind	125	Four Aces	800
Full House	45	Four 2,3,4	400
Flush	30	Four 5-K	250
Straight	20	Full House	45
3-of-a-Kind	15	Flush	35
Two Pair	10	Straight	25
Jacks or Better	5	3-of-a-Kind	15
		Two Pair	5
		Jacks or Better	5

Fig. 11: JACKS OR BETTER

	9/6	8/5	All American	Bonus Poker Deluxe		8/5 Bonus	10/7Dbl Bonus
R. Flush	4000*	4000*	4000	4000	R. Flush	4000	4000
St. Flush	250	250	1000	250	St. Flush	250	250
4-Kind	125	125	200	400	4 Aces	400	800
F. House	45	40	40	40	4 2,3,4	200	400
Flush	30	25	40	25	5-K	125	250
Straight	20	20	40	20	F. House	40	50
3-Kind	15	15	15	15	Flush	25	35
Two-Pair	10	10	10	5	Straight	20	25
Pair	5	5	5	5	3-Kind	15	15
Theoretical Return:	99.5%	97.3%	100.7%	99.0%	Two-Pair	10	5
					Pair	5	5
					Theoretical Return:	99.2%	100.15%

*If progressive, 100% return at $1250 for 9/6, $2380, and $2950 for 7/5.

©copyright, 1999 The GameMaster Online, Inc.

7/5 Bonus returns 98%.
9/7 Double Bonus returns 99.0%

The tables in this example show the payouts for games in which five coins are played. The table on the left represents a "9/6 Jacks or Better" game. We know this because the full house (when dividing the payout by 5) pays 9 for 1 and the flush pays 6 for 1. It is, therefore, a "9/6" game. It's a "Jacks or Better" game because the lowest hand that pays is a pair of Jacks. Through computer-generated analysis, it can be determined that such a game has a long-term return of 99.54%. If you see a similar game, but the full house pays only 40 (8 for 1) and the flush pays 25 (5 for 1), then you're looking at an "8/5 Jacks or Better" game, and it has a long-term return of 97.3% (not so great).

You might also run across a game, like the table on the right, in which the full house pays 45 and the flush pays 35. At a glance you might think you've found a very generous jacks game, but before loading it up with cyber tokens, notice the rest of the schedule is different from that of the table on the left. The table on the right is a 9/7 Double Bonus, and it has a long-term return of only 99.1%. The "full-pay" version of Double Bonus is in a 10/7 format, and its pay schedule returns 100.15%.

So it's all clear, yes? If you're in the majority, your response to this explanation was something along the lines of, "Huh?" There are means of calculating these payout schedules with 100% accuracy and if you're ambitious and number-hungry enough, you can get to

Fig. 12: DEUCES WILD

	Full-Pay	Pay	Double	Triple
R. Flush	4000	4000	4000	4000
4 Deuces	1000	1000	2000	3000
Wild Royal	125	125	100	100
5-Kind	75	75	50	50
St. Flush	45	45	50	40
4-Kind	25	20	20	20
Full House	15	20	20	15
Flush	10	15	15	10
Straight	10	10	10	10
3-Kind	5	5	5	5
Theoretical Return:	100.6%	98.0%	101%	100%

©copyright, 1999 The GameMaster Online, Inc.

Fig. 13: JOKER WILD

	Full-Pay	Short-Pay	Two-Pair	Low-Pay
Royal Flush	4000	4000	5000	4000
5-of-a-Kind	1000	1000	500	500
Wild Royal	500	500	250	250
St. Flush	250	250	250	250
4-of-a-Kind	100	75	100	80
Full House	35	35	40	40
Flush	25	25	35	35
Straight	15	15	25	25
3-of-a-Kind	10	10	10	10
Two Pairs	5	5	5	5
K or Better	5	5	0	0
Theoretical Return:	100.6%	96.3%	99.1%	95.5%

©copyright, 1999 The GameMaster Online, Inc.

Fig. 14: BONUS POKER

	Bonus	Double Bonus	Full House	Super Aces
Royal Flush	4000	4000	4000	4000
St. Flush	250	250	500	250
4 Aces	400	800	1000	2000
4 2,3,4	200	400	200	400
4 5-K	125	250	125	250
Full House	40	50	60	40
Flush	25	35	40	25
Straight	20	25	25	20
3-of-a-Kind	15	15	15	15
Two Pairs	10	5	5	5
Pair of Jacks	5	5	5	5
Theoretical Return:	99.2%	100.1%	99.3%	99.8%

©copyright, 1999 The GameMaster Online, Inc.

Fig. 15: DOUBLE POKER

	Double Bonus	Double Bonus Plus		Double-Double Jackpot	Double Bonus Jackpot		Double-Double Bonus
Royal Flush	4000	4000	Royal Flush	4000	4000	Royal Flush	4000
St. Flush	250	250	Straight Flush	250	250	Straight Flush	250
4 Aces	800	800	4 Aces + Face	1600	800	4 Aces + 2,3,4"	2000
4 2,3,4	400	400	4 Aces	800	400	4 Aces	800
4 5-K	250	250	4 Faces + Ace/Face	800	400	Four 2,3, 4 + A,2,3,4	800
Full House	50	40	4 Faces	400	200	Four 2,3,4	400
Flush	35	25	4 2-10	250	100	Four 5-King	250
Straight	25	20	Full House	50	40	Full House	45
3-of-a-Kind	15	10	Flush	30	25	Flush	30
Two pairs	5	10	Straight	20	20	Straight	20
Js or Better	5	5	3-of-a-Kind	15	15	3-of-a-Kind	15
Theoretical Return:	100.1%	99.5%	Two pairs	5	10	Two pairs.	5
			Js or Better	5	5	Js or Better	5
			Theoretical Return:	100.3%	99.4%	Theoretical Return:	98.8%

©copyright, 1999 The GameMaster Online, Inc.

Dispelling a Myth

Casino gamblers love to flock to "hot" machines, whether it's on the Internet or at a bricks-and-mortar casino. This is complete garbage when it comes to playing video poker. The first key to winning is finding a game that pays well, but this has nothing to do whether the game is "hot" or "cold." Legitimate video poker software deals the cards randomly, so as long as the rules are the same from one game to other, so are the odds. The pay schedule is all that matters.

As stated, these payout schedules only apply when perfect strategy is used. So the next step, then, is learning proper strategy. This is easier then you might think, as video poker is like blackjack in that there is one right move in every circumstance. There are numerous books available, and that's nice, but herein lays the beauty of Internet gambling. As long as you're gambling in the digital world, why not hire a digital coach? There are a handful of software applications—available for purchase online—that teach perfect video poker strategy and allow you to practice right there at your computer. One such program is "Bob Dancer Presents WinPoker," by Zamzow Software Solutions and it's available at www.zamzone.com. Of course, if you're not interested in "learning" proper strategy there is always the proverbial cheat sheet, which you can keep on your desktop and reference as you play online. Printed strategy cards are available online at www.jazbo.com and other video poker-oriented sites. You can also make your own by purchasing "Video Poker Strategy Master," a software application available at online stores such as www.conjelco.com.

the bottom of it, but the purpose of showing these tables is simply to illustrate how video poker games vary. Assuming that you're in majority—those who aren't interested in number crunching—then all you need to know is which games pay better and leave it at that. Figures 12, 13, 14, 15 (pages 49 & 50) show payout schedules for common video poker games. You can commit them to memory or commit them to a cheat sheet, but either way, you should be aware of the numbers before you partake in any game of video poker (unless, of course, you're more interested in how pretty the game looks than you are winning money, in which case, disregard this entire chapter!)

The Long-Term Outlook

The reality of video poker is that you'll have more losing sessions than winning sessions. Even when using proper strategy for a game that pays out better than 100%, you must keep in mind that profit in video poker doesn't happen on a regular and consistent basis. You might have a half-dozen losing sessions in a row and then see a couple of sessions with big wins. In the long term, you can pretty much guarantee that you'll realize a profit from video poker if you follow three very important guidelines:

- Play games with pay schedules offering a long-term return of over 100%.
- Always use proper playing strategy.
- Have adequate finances to cover inevitable short-term losses.

The Online Experience

Online video poker, from a strategy standpoint, pretty much replicates the bricks-and-mortar experience. Perhaps the biggest difference is that land-based video poker machines often pay out more than 100%, whereas online video poker almost never does. There is a simple explanation for this: At the beginning of this section I explained that casinos can profit from video poker machines that pay out better than 100% because they can always count on less-than-perfect strategy—and lots of it. The digital world is different. Just as the games are offered in an automated manner, they can be played in an automated manner. There's nothing to stop a programmer, for example, from creating software that plays video poker using perfect strategy and using that software to get an edge at an online casino. All he has to do is let the software play hand after hand after hand, and he will see a profit over time. The creators of online casino software realize that they can't always count on "user error" as the bricks-and-mortar folks do, so they have maintained the house edge.

But there's good news! Some online casinos offer video poker games that pay out just under 100%, and when you add to that the cash you get back through players clubs, you can push the edge back in your favor. InterCasino's Double Bonus poker, for example, has a return of 99.94% and offers players 0.10% cash back for

their play. Now here's a piece of math that's actually easy to understand (for a change): Add the cash back you receive to the equation and the return is bumped to 100.04%. Voila, we have an edge for the player.

Another way to tip the scale in your favor is to play progressive games. A video poker game with a return of 98% to 99% as a standalone game pushes the edge in your favor as a progressive game once the jackpot reaches a certain point. Keep in mind, though, that the progressive is won by hitting a royal flush and that you have to be committed—and willing to lose money in the short term—to make it work for you. Slotcharts.com is a great place to monitor online progressive jackpots. Click "Video Poker Games Ranked by Return" in the

InterCasino's Double Bonus video poker game has a return rate of more than 100% if you play perfect strategy and take advantage of their player rewards program.

Home

Best Jackpots Right Now:
(Ranked every 5 minutes)
#1: LotsaLoot
#2: Jack in the Box (50c)
#3: Light Speed
#4: Card Shark
#5: Caribbean Stud Poker ($/€)
        More...

See all the games:
  Grouped by software
  Ranked by score

See recent jackpots won.

See all the casinos.

Video Poker Games,
Ranked by Return

By Software:
Boss Media
Cryptologic
Global Player
MicroGaming
OddsOn
PlayTech
SlotLand

Bookmark us now!

Let us keep you up-to-date with
the latest features.

Video Poker Progressives

Games are listed in order of theoretical payback, at the current progressive values.

Click on a game to see more details and links to the casinos.

Game	Software	Jackpot	Current Return
Royal Diamond	888.com	$ 27,855.11	100.27 %
Jacks or Better VP 25c	Global Player	$ 1,659.72	99.67 %
Double Joker VP 50c	Global Player	$ 3,667.04	99.58 %
Bonus Deluxe VP $1	Global Player	$ 5,620.40	99.26 %
Deuces & Joker VP 5c	Global Player	$ 675.13	99.22 %
Quick Pick VP 3-Line 5c	Global Player	$ 1,186.03	99.16 %
Super Jackpot (0.25 $/£/€)	Cryptologic	$ 1,622.34	98.54 %
Sevens Wild VP 50c	Global Player	$ 2,738.01	98.52 %
Double Double Bonus VP 25c	Global Player	$ 1,160.96	98.48 %
Jacks or Better VP 3-Line 5c	Global Player	$ 209.23	98.45 %
Super Jackpot (1 $/£/€)	Cryptologic	$ 6,266.92	98.43 %
Dbl Dbl Bonus VP 3-Line 25c	Global Player	$ 1,092.87	98.35 %
Loose Deuces VP 50c	Global Player	$ 2,394.63	98.34 %
Mega Jacks	PlayTech	$ 358.20	98.27 %
Deuces & Joker VP 3-Line 10c	Global Player	$ 691.95	98.26 %
Jackpot Deuces	MicroGaming	$ 33,893.28	97.73 %
Jackpot Video Poker	Boss Media	$ 33,138.08	97.46 %

Wanna know where the hot games are? SlotCharts.com keeps updated lists of the progressive video poker games with the highest returns.

left column and get list of progressive video poker games with updated return rates.

Once you find a game that pays back better than 100%, you'll realize how the speed of Internet gambling can work to your advantage. Considering that you have to play a heck of a lot of games of video poker to realize an edge, that you can play video poker online twice as quickly as you can at a land-based casino and thus reap the reward of having an edge much sooner. Before you're off to the races though, consider these two things: 1.) Playing more games an hour means you'd better be prepared to absorb bigger losses in the short term before your play pays off; and 2.) Playing at lightning speed makes you much more susceptible to making errors.

ONLINE POKER

You can play at a casino, you can play
at home. You can watch live on
television, and now you can play
poker online with people from
around the world.

ONLINE POKER

"Why does this still seem like gambling to you? I mean, why do you think the same five guys make it to the final table of the World Series of Poker every single year? What, are they the luckiest guys in Las Vegas? It's a skill game..." – Matt Damon, *Rounders* (1998)

And with that, the message to millions of moviegoers was made clear: Intelligence, not luck, wins poker games. Add to the mix venues accessible to anyone with an Internet connection, throw in a few celebrity aficionados, and the recipe for a craze was born.

The History of Poker

Depending on who you ask, the game of poker can be traced back to origins as diverse as France, China, and even ancient Persia. Most likely though, modern poker evolved out of the elements of many different games.

Poker forever embedded itself in American culture during the early 1800s where it was first played on

Mississippi riverboats. Evidence of this comes in the words of famous American writer (and former riverboat pilot), Mark Twain, who commented, "Why, I have known clergymen, good men, kind-hearted, liberal, sincere, and all that, who did not know the meaning of a "flush". It is enough to make one ashamed of one's species."

In addition to the riverboats, poker spread throughout the United States by way of wagon train and rail. Games played in the saloons of the Wild West included participants such as the ruthless lawman, James Butler "Wild Bill" Hickok. A charter member of the Poker Hall of Fame at Binion's Horseshoe Casino in Las Vegas, Hickok was shot in the back of the head during a poker game on August 2, 1876 in the town of Deadwood, South Dakota. The hand he was holding at the time of his death consisted of pairs of aces and eights, known forever after as the "Dead Man's Hand."

Poker continued to evolve into the twentieth century, and with the legalisation of gambling in the state of Nevada in 1931, the game found a safe haven in the highly regulated world of casinos.

In 1970, the World Series of Poker was created by Benny Binion to be held at his casino in Las Vegas. The WSOP continues to this day as the pinnacle event for the world's top poker players, and many allude to this widely televised tournament as a key contributor to the recent rise of interest in poker.

Also contributing to poker's skyrocketing popularity today is a host of celebrities who have taken up the

Most online poker rooms offer several features to enhance the playing experience.

game. Included in this group are stars Ben Affleck, Tobey Maguire, James Woods, and Leonardo DiCaprio.

But most point to the creation of online poker as the catalyst for the current craze. In 2003, Chris Moneymaker won his seat to the WSOP via an online tournament with an entrance fee of $40. It is a popular myth that he had never played in a live tournament, but Moneymaker would go on to be crowned the 2003 WSOP champion, earning $2,500,000 in the process. It was a true Cinderella story and would motivate countless others to try their hands at poker. After all, if an online amateur could win it all, what was stopping them?

Playing Poker Online

Sitting down at a live poker game can be very intimidating for the newly initiated player. Not only does one have to concentrate on the game at hand, but there are also betting procedures and table etiquette to be mindful of. Combine this with the fact that the other players at the table are not exactly going to go out of their way to make the amateur feel more comfortable and it is no wonder that most poker beginners today go online to get acquainted with the game.

In addition to the intimidation factor, there are many other advantages that amateurs and experts alike see in playing online, including the following:

PLAY-MONEY GAMES – A good way to learn the rules and betting procedures of poker is to compete in play-money games. No deposit.

LOWER RAKE AND NO DEALER TIPS – Poker room operators make money by charging a rake, or commission, on each hand, typically a percentage of each pot. With less overhead costs, most online poker rooms can charge lower rakes than real life poker rooms. Dealer tips, generally a dollar or two for each large pot won, are also a non-factor online.

BONUSES AND FREEROLLS – Also due to their lower overhead expenses, online poker rooms can afford to offer enticing bonuses and/or freerolls (tournaments with no entry fees, with prize money put up by the site) to new or frequent players.

MORE HANDS PER HOUR – Because the dealing, shuffling of cards and betting is instantaneous, online games are played at a much faster rate, approximately twice as fast as a live game.

WIDE SELECTION OF GAME TYPES, STAKE SIZES, AT ANY TIME – You can find all your favourite poker games at any hour of the day online. You can play regular games, tournaments, or heads-up (one-on-one) games for stakes as low as $0.01 per bet and as high as no limit at all.

PLAYER STATISTICS AND OPPONENT NOTES – Online software allows you to chart useful statistics such as how much you win (or lose) per hour, what percent of hands you see the flop with, and what percent of pots you win at the showdown. It also allows you to enter notes on your opponents for future reference.

Finding the Online Poker Room that's Right for You

It is highly advisable to do your research before signing up with an online poker site. The site should be licensed, should possess a solid reputation within the online

gaming community, and should offer reliable customer service 24 hours a day, 365 days a year.

If you find a site that satisfies the above prerequisites, you can download their software and try partaking in some play money games to get acquainted with the technology.

Finally, before you deposit any money, try striking up a chat with some of the site's players to ask them what they think of the site and whether or not they have received their pay-outs without incident.

The Different Games of Poker

Over the years, countless versions of poker have evolved. Summarised below are the types you are most likely to find offered online.

TEXAS HOLD 'EM is far and away the most popular poker game out there today. The game concept itself is pretty simple. Each player is dealt two cards face down (called

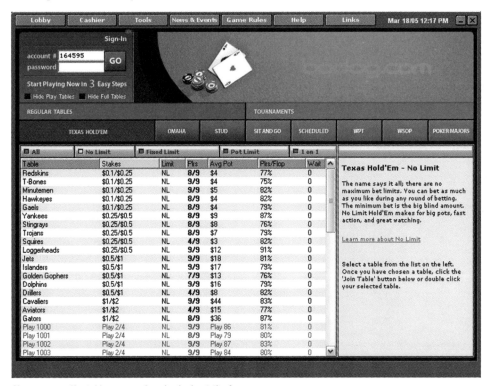

Choose yourself a table once you've checked out the form.

"pocket cards"). The dealer then deals five community cards face up; these are available to all the players to help make their hand. Players may use any combination of their pocket cards and the community cards to make their hand. The best five-card hand takes the pot.

OMAHA and Texas Hold 'em are played the same way, except that in Omaha, instead of two pocket cards face down, each player starts with four. The game is then played exactly the same as Hold 'em, with the exception of the showdown. At the showdown players must use two (only two) of their four cards in combination with three (only three) of the community cards to create the best five-card hand.

OMAHA HI/LO – The premise for Omaha Hi/Lo is that there are two winning hands for each game: the strongest (highest) hand and the weakest (lowest) hand split the pot. For a hand to qualify as a low hand, it cannot have any card higher than an 8. And because Aces count both as a high card and as a low card, the best possible low hand is A, 2, 3, 4 and 5. Although you're probably thinking, "Isn't that a straight?" And you'd be right, except that in Omaha Hi/Lo, any hand that qualifies for the low is not affected by straights or flushes. This creates an interesting situation: You can qualify for both the highest and the lowest hand in a game. If you win both, you take the whole pot.

SEVEN-CARD STUD – In Seven-Card Stud, each player is dealt two face-down "hole cards", and one face up "door card." The dealer then deals to each player in turn three more face up cards, and one more face-down card. The player with the highest five-card hand takes the pot.

SEVEN-CARD STUD HIGH-LOW – As with Omaha High-Low, players seek either the highest or lowest hand, or both.

FIVE-CARD STUD – In Five-Card Stud, players are dealt one hole card, and one door card. The dealer then deals to each player in turn three more face up cards. The player with the highest five-card hand takes the pot.

Betting Procedures

ANTES AND BLINDS are both forced bets required by players before any cards are dealt. An ante is contributed by each player while a blind is only required of certain players. For example, in Hold 'em, the "small blind" is made by the player immediately to the left of the dealer button and is equal to half of the minimum bet, rounded

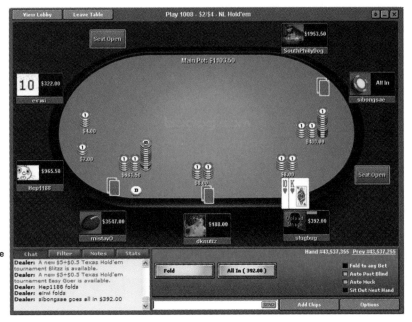

The online player never bets the wrong amount or out of turn. The software will prompt you when it's your turn and gives you all your options.

down to the nearest dollar. Subsequently, the "big blind" is made by the player immediately to the left of the small blind, and is equal to the minimum bet.

BETTING ACTIONS – A round of betting ensues whenever players receive new cards. Players take turns betting, going in a clockwise order, usually beginning with the player to the immediate left of the dealer, or the "button". (After each hand, the button moves clockwise to the next active player, who becomes the dealer for that hand.)

In Hold 'em and Omaha, the first player to act in any round of betting has two options:

- CHECK: If a player checks, he or she is declining to make the first bet and, instead, is passing that option onto the next player in the betting sequence.
- BET: A bet occurs when a player puts an amount of money into the pot.

Once a bet has been placed in the pot, all subsequent players in the betting round are given the following three options:

- FOLD: If a player elects to fold, he or she withdraws from the hand and forfeits all of his or her bets (including antes or blinds) placed up to that point in the hand.

- CALL: To call a bet, a player matches the amount the player preceding them in the betting sequence has placed in the pot.

- RAISE: A player raises by matching and exceeding an amount bet by a player earlier in the betting sequences. Should a player raise, all players must meet this new amount to remain in the hand.

BETTING LIMITS – There are three limit-type games: Fixed Limit, Pot Limit, and No Limit.

In a Fixed Limit game, both the bet and raise amounts for each round are a predetermined amount. For example, in a $5/$10 Fixed game, both the bets and raises for the first two rounds of betting must be $5, no more, no less. The last two rounds have a bet/raise amount of $10. In addition, each round of betting may

consist of a maximum number of allowable raises, known as the "cap".

In a Pot Limit game, the maximum bet/raise cannot be more than the current pot amount.

The final game type is No Limit. The name says it all; there are no maximum bet limits.

BETTING ROUNDS—Tying the above together, the following examines the four different rounds of betting in a game of Hold 'em:

- PRE FLOP: After the deal (two cards face down), the next player after the big blind decides whether to call, raise or fold the big blind. Each player in turn is given these options, until all bets are called and the big blind checks. In a fixed limit game, any raises are limited to the lower stake amount.

- THE FLOP: The dealer turns over the first three community cards. All betting rounds start with the player directly to the dealers left. For fixed limit games, this round of betting still uses the lower stake.

- THE TURN: Also known as "fourth street", the fourth community card is dealt, and a new betting round begins. The bet amount in our fixed limit game increases to the upper stake.

- THE RIVER: Here the final community card is shown, and the last round of betting takes place. The bet amount for fixed limit games is still the upper stake.

The Showdown—After all the bets have been called, it's time to show the cards. The best five card hand, "the nuts", takes the pot, determined in accordance with the hand rankings below.

Hand Rankings
ROYAL FLUSH

Ace, King, Queen, Jack and Ten, all in the same suit.

STRAIGHT FLUSH

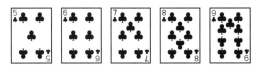

Five cards in numerical sequence, all in the same suit. If two or more exist at showdown, the highest ranked card at the top of the sequence wins the pot.

FOUR OF A KIND

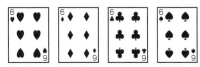

Four cards of the same rank with the fifth card being the highest eligible card. If two or more exist in a hand, the highest four of a kind wins.

FULL HOUSE (AKA—"BOAT")

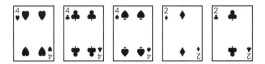

Three cards of matching rank with two cards of different matching rank. If two or more exist at showdown, the highest three matching cards wins.

FLUSH

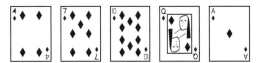

Five cards of matching suit. If two or more exist in a hand, the highest ranked card wins.

STRAIGHT

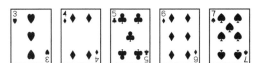

Five cards in ranked sequence. If two or more exist at showdown, the highest ranked card at the top of the sequence wins the pot.

THREE OF A KIND (AKA – "SET" OR "TRIPS")

Three cards of matching rank with two cards of different ranks. If two or more exist at showdown, the highest ranking three of a kind wins. If players have the same three matching cards, the highest ranked fourth (or fifth when necessary) card wins.

TWO PAIR

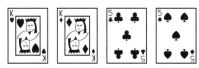

Two cards of matching rank with two additional cards of a different matching rank. The fifth card is an unrelated rank. If two or more exist at showdown, the highest pair wins. If both pairs are identical, the highest fifth card by rank wins.

ONE PAIR

Two cards of matching rank with three additional cards of unrelated ranks. If two or more exist at showdown, the highest pair wins. If pairs of the same rank exist, the highest ranked unrelated card wins.

HIGH CARD

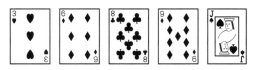

Five cards that are not of the same suit, are not ranked sequentially and uniquely ranked. If two or more exist at showdown, the highest ranked card wins.

Tournaments

Playing in a tournament offers the chance to play a lot of poker for a small entry fee. And with some smart play and a little bit of luck, even a beginner can win a large pot every now and then. Because of this, tournaments have become increasingly popular online and are available in a wide array of styles and formats, as summarized below:

MULTI-TABLE TOURNAMENTS – Players start multi-table tournaments with a fixed number of chips and play until one player has all the chips. Blinds and antes increase as the tournament progresses, and as players are eliminated tables are consolidated together. The number of tables is eventually reduced to one final table. The total sum of all the entry fees is divided up and awarded to the top players in accordance with the tournament's previously determined split.

SATELLITES – Satellites are tournaments designed to allow players to win seats to bigger tournaments for a fraction of the buy-in. A multi-table tournament may have several satellites that players may enter to win a seat at the bigger event.

RE-BUY TOURNAMENTS – A typical multi-table tournament has only one buy-in and once a player is out of chips they are finished for the tournament. Re-Buy tournaments are different from traditional multi-table tournaments in that they allow players to purchase additional chips during the course of the tournament.

SIT 'N' GO TOURNAMENTS – A Sit n' Go is a mini-tournament that does not begin at a designated time, but rather when all the seats are filled.

Etiquette

As at a live poker table, a standard degree of etiquette is expected and enforced when playing online.

GAME CHAT – Chatting at the table is one of the enjoyable aspects of playing poker. Friendly chat and banter are certainly a fun part of the game, but abusive or profane chat is not. Bad beats are a reality of poker, and you should resist the urge to use the chat box as a method of venting your frustration.

ENGLISH ONLY – In the interest of protecting everyone from collusion and team play, only English is allowed at most online sites.

LET THE CARDS SPEAK – Players should refrain from commenting during a hand on cards they have folded, or expressing disappointment as the cards are dealt. This is to prevent players from inferring from the chat about what cards may have helped or hurt the chances of other players.

TIMELY AND COURTEOUS PLAY – An important part of poker is making intelligent decisions, and you are certainly allowed to take a moment to consider your actions; however, you should generally aspire to play at a reasonable pace.

COLLUSION – For as long as there has been poker, there has been collusion. Collusion is when two or more players communicate information about their hands during the course of play. The best way to avoid being victimised by collusion is to play at a site with a solid reputation and brand name to protect. To ensure that customers continue playing at their site, they will be strongly committed to detecting all forms of collusion. Remember that online sites log every hand played on their site and can easily track the betting patterns of players suspected of collusion.

Beginner Strategy

GAME SELECTION – The difference between starting your poker career off as a winner or as a loser is Game Selection. Choose the appropriate game for your bankroll and skill level and you will be rewarded with a long and rewarding poker life.

BANKROLL – Make sure you have an adequate bankroll for the stakes of the game; about 200 times the big bet should suffice (e.g. $200 to play at $.50/$1).

EVALUATE THE GAME – Some games are tougher than others are, even though the limits are the same. Take some time to observe a game before sitting down.

TIGHT/LOOSE AND PASSIVE/AGGRESSIVE – There are two major ways to describe games and players: Tight/Loose and Passive/Aggressive. Tight/Loose describes how many hands a player will play. If they play very few hands, then they are considered Tight. If they play a lot of hands, then they are considered Loose. Passive/Aggressive describes how often players tend to bet their hands. Passive players do not bet very often and prefer to call or check. Aggressive players tend to heavily bet their hands and rarely call or check. The easiest and most profitable games are those that are Loose/Passive, where players tend to play too many weak hands, and do not raise often enough when they have strong hands.

Your position at the table is simply your position in relation to the dealer and to other players who are active in a particular pot. The dealer is at the most advantageous position, as he/she can wait to see how all the players at the table react before making their own decision, but even if you're not the dealer it is important to take note of your position in terms of betting strategy.

Don't forget to observe: One of the great advantages of playing poker online is the ability to keep notes on all your opponents, which you can refer to during future sessions.

POSITION – "Early" Position is defined as the first three players to act after the blinds (for a full table of ten). A player in early position should only play strong hands, as there are players to act after them who may raise.

Middle Position, the next three players, may play slightly weaker hands than an early position player may as they have the opportunity to see some of the action before them.

Late Position, the last two players, may play a greater number of hands, as they are able to see the actions of the majority of the players at the table.

BLINDS – The blinds have the advantage of playing a diverse number of hands as they have already contributed either a partial or full bet. If there is a raise before them, then the blinds must often fold, as they will be in Early Position after the flop and will thus need a strong hand to continue.

Hand Selection

The hands mentioned here are just a rough guide. Playing more hands than this list suggests is perfectly fine if a player is comfortable with the action of the game.

Note: Suited cards are stronger than unsuited cards as they also have the possibility of making a flush.

EARLY POSITION

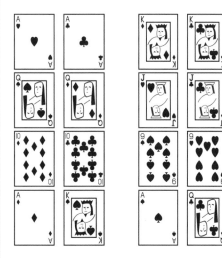

MIDDLE POSITION

LATE POSITION

BLINDS – In an un-raised pot: The same hands as Middle and Late Position.

In a raised pot: The same hands as Early Position.

FOLDING – A good player will fold far more hands than they will play. You should generally fold before the flop any hand not listed above, and/or if the flop does not pair your high card(s), make three of kind, or flop two cards

to a straight or flush. You should also usually fold if the betting actions of another player(s) convince you that you are beaten, or if you do not complete your straight or flush draws after the last community card is dealt.

CHECKING – You should always consider raising or folding before checking. However, you should typically check if the community cards have not helped you. Drawing hands can also be checked in the hopes of seeing the next card for free. Further, if you are unsure of whether or not you have the best hand at the showdown, then checking is often the best course of action.

CALLING – Again, be sure to seriously consider raising or folding before calling. Drawing hands are often worth calling in the hopes of making a straight or a flush. That said, drawing hands usually require a slightly bigger pot or more players in the hand to make them worthwhile playing out. Same as checking, if you are unsure of whether or not you have the best hand at the showdown, then simply calling is the prudent play.

BETTING/RAISING/RE-RAISING/CHECKRAISING – A player should bet, raise, or re-raise whenever they believe that they have the best hand. This is done to increase the amount of the bets in the pot and/or to induce those with drawing hands to fold. Players in late position may also bet or raise with strong drawing hands to either win the pot right away, or to enable them to receive a "free" card on the next betting round when all the players who act before them check. If a player flops or later makes a very strong hand, then checkraising (checking first and then raising when a player behind you bets) becomes a powerful play to get extra bets into the pot.

BLUFFING – (betting with a weak hand in order to induce others to fold) is an important part of poker. Bluffing can often win pots, and it allows players to create deception and uncertainty in the minds of their opponents. Bluffing works better against a smaller number of opponents, since with a larger number of opponents, one of them is bound to call you. Avoid bluffing "calling stations" (players who tend to call too much) and be mindful of bluffing too much, as your opponents will soon catch on.

OBSERVE YOUR OPPONENTS – A winning poker player will constantly be observing their fellow players. Analysing an opponent's play allows a player insight into what hand their competitors may hold. A player should pay attention to other players and their actions even when not involved in the hand.

INCREASE YOUR KNOWLEDGE – Finally, the above information covers only the basics. As you gain experience in poker, you must also commit yourself to increasing your knowledge of the game. A large part of every poker player's arsenal should be a collection of books. *The Theory of Poker* by David Sklansky, *Winning Low-Limit Hold'em* by Lee Jones, and *Super System* by Doyle Brunson are three books that should comprise part of your poker library.

my account | deposit | payout | logout

POKER

PLAY NOW
- Download
- Getting Started
- Quick Tour

RULES
- Texas Holdem
- Omaha
- Omaha High Low
- 7 Card Stud
- 7 Card Stud High Low
- 5 Card Stud
- Game Limits

TOURNAMENTS
- Tournament Leader Board
- World Poker Tour
- World Series of Poker
- $100K Guaranteed
- Daily Tournaments
- Tournament Types
- Tournament Rules
- Tournament Schedule

HOW TO PLAY
- Beginner Strategy
- Guide to Playing Poker
- Etiquette
- Play Money

GAME INFO
- Bodog Poker Points
- Rake
- Game Fairness

GETTING STARTED

STEP 1. Open an account

Open an account

Already have an account? Proceed to Step 2.

STEP 2. Download & Install

Download Bodog Poker Room

The software will automatically run after installation. In the future, you can get to Bodog Poker at anytime by double-clicking the **Bodog Poker icon** on your desktop.

STEP 3. Select Screen Name

Set up a Bodog Poker account by choosing a screen name and filling in the required information. The name you select will be used to identify you in the Bodog Community. Establishing an account does not signify a financial or binding commitment to Bodog, and is solely used to enable a player to play on the Bodog website.

STEP 4. Select Player Image

Another way to personalize your identity at Bodog Poker is to add a player image. This image will be displayed along with your selected screen name while seated at a table. To add your image, click the **'Tools'** button at the top of the main lobby window of the software, and then click the **'Select / Edit Player Image'** item from the menu list. A new window will open that will let you select an image saved on your computer to use as a display image at the tables. For complete instructions, please visit the Player Images page of our website.

Play Money

All new accounts at Bodog Poker are automatically credited with 1,000 play chips and are ready for play at our Play Money Tables. If your play money balance drops below 500, you may add an additional 1,000 play money chips by clicking on the **'Cashier'** button in the main lobby window and then select

SPORTSBOOK

Whatever sport or bet type is your passion; Bodog takes you front and center with fast and easy betting.

Enter Sportsbook Now

Enter Racebook Now

CASINO

Large progressive jackpots. $1 table game minimums. WinAMillion slot! Cash in with 50+ Vegas style games. Learn More

Download

Getting Started

LOUNGE

Visit the Bodog Lounge for the latest Bodog columns, contest details, and breaking news. Plus check out the latest adventures of the Bodog Girls.

Most web sites will make your route to a poker game a simple one. The BoDog.com site walks players through the process of getting started.

ONLINE SPORTS BETTING

Horses, football, bat and stick games—
you can watch them all on television
and place all sorts of bets online.

ONLINE SPORTS BETTING

For as long as there have been sports, there have been sports fans eager to bet on the results. Fast forward to the 21st century where there are more events being televised through regular television, cable and satellite technology than ever before, and you can easily understand why there's such a huge interest. Increased marketing and promotion of professional and collegiate sports are not to be overlooked, but the single most contributing factor has been the Internet.

Sports betting has enjoyed a much longer run in the mainstream market in the United Kingdom, with bricks-and-mortar betting shops almost everywhere, making it as commonplace as beans on toast. In that respect, American sports bettors have had some catching up to do, but as the numbers continue to rise in both the UK and US, it is crystal clear that sports betting has taken on a truly global appeal. And it took the Internet to keep us connected.

The Internet has revolutionized sports betting, making it easier and faster for you to place wagers on your favorite teams or games taking place in your hometown or halfway around the world. The Internet has literally put a world of sports and betting information and round-the-clock access to your accounts at your fingertips. The convenience factor alone has resulted in a dramatic growth in online sports betting, and it has created an industry that is estimated to bring in over $60 billion per year worldwide.

Differences between Sports Betting in the United Kingdom and the United States

Even though they may never bet against their favorite team, it is still believed that on average, UK bettors are sharper than their American counterparts. There is simply nothing in American sports, or American culture for that matter, that draws the same amount of interest as a major soccer game being played in the United Kingdom.

The differences between the two groups of bettors may have much to do with the games themselves and how they're played. In the United States, American football, baseball, and basketball are favorites among all sports bettors. Football (soccer), rugby and cricket rank high among punters in the United Kingdom.

In the UK, league games are decided over 90 minutes of play with no extra time if the teams are tied. So your team can win, lose or tie the game. A tie signals a draw and frequently two sets of odds are given. In the US, where scores for football and basketball games are rather high in comparison, there isn't any opportunity for a draw (with the rare exception of scoreless sudden-death overtime in the NFL, which happens maybe once or twice a year).

Another big difference is the way the lines are expressed. In the US, they use the moneyline system. With the moneyline, the favorite and underdog are given odds to win a game or event. The minus sign (e.g. −130) always indicates the favorite and the amount you must bet ($130) to win ($100). The plus sign (e.g. +120) always indicates the underdog or outsider and the amount that you win ($120) for every bet ($100). In Europe and Asia the most commonly price system is the decimal. This provides the simplest way of calculating your total return, i.e. your winnings including your stake. All you have to do is multiply your stake by the decimal price given (e.g. $10 x 1.90 = $19.00, including your stake).

Online vs. Land-based Sports Betting

Sitting in a huge room looking at hundreds of lines and dozens of screens while being served ice-cold beverages definitely makes sports betting at land-based sports books appealing, but online sports books have their advantages, too. With online sports books, there are no face-to-face transactions, and that means there are also no line-ups. While Las Vegas sports books can process about 20 to 30 clients at a time, Internet sports books can process thousands simultaneously. And because there is no need to have people on hand to personally process every bet, the Internet sports books have much lower costs per wager. And they can pass this type of savings on to the bettor in the form of deposit bonuses or reduced juice (commission taken by the bookmaker).

The Internet also enables bettors to shop for the best possible lines very quickly. Going from the Mirage to Bally's to the Bellagio to Mandalay Bay in Las Vegas to

shop for lines would take at least an hour, but you can check the lines at dozens of Internet sports books in mere seconds.

Online sports betting gives punters greater accessibility to information and wagering opportunities

bodog | SPORTSBOOK CASINO POKER LOUNGE   service@bodog.com

EXPERIENCE THE THRILL
OF ONLINE SPORTS,
CASINO, AND POKER

Sign-In
account #:
password: GO

my account | deposit | payout | logout

SPORTSBOOK

- Sportsbook
- Open Bets
- Bet History
- Enter Racebook Now

PLAYER TIPS

To place a single, just click on the line of your choice or select the checkbox next to the line you want and click the "Single" button at the top.

For more excitement try a parlay or teaser, just click on the checkboxes next to the lines you want, and then click the "Parlay" or "Teaser" button.

To place cross-sport parlays and teasers, select a sport from the drop-down menu, make your pick, select "Add to Picks", choose your next sport or event and repeat to build your pick list. Once your list is complete, you can combine your picks by clicking on the checkboxes next to each pick, then choose "Parlay" or "Teaser".

NBA BASKETBALL LINES AT BODOG SPORTSBOOK

All Times Eastern Mon Mar. 7, 1:04:31p ET

Select A Sport | Single | Parlay | Teaser | Add to Picks | Update Lines

Mon, Mar 7, 05		Spread	Moneyline		Total		Score
7:35p	**Game can be seen on Comcast**				Matchup | Preview | Injuries		
761	Philadelphia 76ers	+6½	+240	203	Over		
762	Miami Heat	-6½	-280		Under		
8:35p	**Game can be seen on FOX-North**				Matchup | Preview | Injuries		
763	Milwaukee Bucks	+6 (-105)	+230	195	(-115)o		
764	Chicago Bulls	-6 (-115)	-270		(-105)u		
8:35p					Matchup | Preview | Injuries		
765	Toronto Raptors	+5	+190	201	(-105)o		
766	Dallas Mavericks	-5	-230		(-115)u		
9:05p					Matchup | Preview | Injuries		
767	Portland Trail Blazers	+8 (-105)	+300	194	Over		
768	Denver Nuggets	-8 (-115)	-400		Under		
10:35p	**Game can be seen on FOX-Ohio, West**				Matchup | Preview | Injuries		
769	Memphis Grizzlies	+2		181	(-115)o		
770	Los Angeles Clippers	-2			(-105)u		
Tue, Mar 8, 05		Spread	Moneyline		Total		Score
7:05p					Matchup | Preview | Injuries		
801	Golden State Warriors						
802	Philadelphia 76ers						
7:05p					Matchup | Preview | Injuries		
803	Orlando Magic						
804	Cleveland Cavaliers						
7:35p					Matchup | Preview | Injuries		
805	Washington Wizards						
806	New York Knicks						

A screen shot of Bodog.com Sportsbook's NBA basketball lines page. This page also indicates the dates and times of the teams playing. Wagering options available to the bettor shown: spreads, moneylines and totals. The match-up, preview and injury reports are also a click away.

One of the big advantages of betting online is the ease with which you can manage your accounts at online sports books. Online sports bettors can manage their betting activity online in many ways, including viewing betting history, keeping tabs on open bets and closely following their bankrolls.

that are not dependent on location, a wide range of sports to bet on, a number of deposit and withdrawal methods with which to access their accounts, and the ability to bet on multiple events from any computer with Internet access. Web savvy bettors can use the Internet to research teams, find the best odds, register at a sports book and place a wager – all in a fraction of the time it would take them to make the bet at a land-based sports book. But perhaps the best advantage of all is the freedom and convenience that comes from being able to place your wagers from home.

How to Find the Online Sports Book that's Right for You

Choosing an online sports book is about knowing what you want. For some, it's about having a huge selection of sports from which to choose. Other bettors are looking for the site that offers the best bonuses, or one that also

runs its own online casino and/or poker room.

You want a sports book that covers it all, with good sports coverage and competitive odds, and good customer service.

Choosing a sports book is largely a personal preference, but you should look for certain key ingredients when trying to find the one that's right for you:

COMPETITIVE ODDS. Make sure you get the best possible price for each bet. It pays to shop around.

ATTRACTIVE INCENTIVES. Most bettors can appreciate a site that offers at least a few incentives, like sign-up bonuses, referral bonuses and reload bonuses. Look for a site that also offers monthly deposit bonuses or other seasonal promotions.

A GOOD SELECTION OF SPORTING EVENTS AND BETTING OPTIONS. Reputable sports books offer a large selection of events with a wide range of betting options including reverse bets, round robins, futures, propositions

NBA BASKETBALL LINES AT BODOG SPORTSBOOK

All Times Eastern				
Select A Sport ▼	Single	Parlay	Teaser	Add to Picks	Update Lines

Select A Sport
Baseball - Exhibition
Baseball - Futures
Basketball - College First Half
Basketball - College Halftimes
Basketball - College Lines
Basketball - College Props
Basketball - Futures
Basketball - NBA First Halfs
Basketball - NBA Halftimes
Basketball - NBA Lines
Basketball - NBA Props
Film/TV & Politics
Football - Arena Lines
Football - Futures
Horse Racing Props/Futures
Motorsports - Futures
Poker
Soccer - European
Soccer - North American

	Spread	Moneyline	Total	Score
...ES			Matchup | Preview | Injuries	
	+10½(-105) ☐	+425 ☐	190 Over ☐ / Under ☐	
	-10½(-115) ☐	-650 ☐		
...OX-Bay , Turnersouth			Matchup | Preview | Injuries	
	-4 ☐		194 (-105)o ☐ / (-115)u ☐	
	+4 ☐			
			Matchup | Preview | Injuries	
	-6(-115) ☐		194 Over ☐ / Under ☐	
	+6(-105) ☐			
			Matchup | Preview | Injuries	
507 Milwaukee Bucks	Pick ☐		185 Over ☐ / Under ☐	
508 New Orleans Hornets	Pick ☐			

Not only do most online sports books offer a wide variety of betting options, the good ones make it easy to browse those options and make your selections in an uncomplicated virtual environment. BoDog.com, pictured here, takes advantage of scrollable forms.

("props"), straight wagers, parlays, teasers and if bets.

GOOD CUSTOMER SERVICE. This speaks for itself. A sports book that provides knowledgeable and polite customer service is a site that truly respects its customers.

RELEVANT CONTENT. Go with a sports book that is loaded with valuable and relevant information. Sportsbetting often involves a lot of research, and the best sites make that information readily available to its players. Look for free newsletter offers, links to sports-related portals, free picks and other services.

CONVENIENT BANKING OPTIONS. A good sports book should have a few convenient banking options to choose from. For example, NETeller, FirePay, Western Union, credit card and check.

PROFESSIONAL, EASY-TO-FOLLOW LAYOUT. Be very suspicious of sports books that are difficult to navigate and look as though they were thrown together by a junior web designer. This could signal a struggling organization – not one you want to trust with your money.

HISTORY AND REPUTATION. Look for a company that has been in business for a few years and has withstood the test of time.

Understanding the Basics of Sports Betting

Placing a bet on your favorite team or sport event adds an element of excitement to the game you're watching. That could explain why office pools are so popular. When placing your bets through an online sports book, you should also take into consideration a number of other factors, but the main object is simple: Beat the oddsmakers and win some money. How and where you place your bets is an entirely different ballgame and the process can be a bit daunting for the beginner, but it helps to start with an understanding of the different types of bets that can be placed (at any number of sports books throughout the United Kingdom and the United States). Here is a good starting list:

FAVORITES, UNDERDOGS, AND HOME TEAMS – When two teams or players compete in any event, usually one of the two will be expected or "favored" to win; this competitor will be considered the favorite and the other, not expected to win, will be the underdog. The team that hosts the game will be considered the home team (generally on the bottom) and the team which travels to play the game, will be called the visitor.

LINES – MONEYLINE - A line structured on a $100 basis; to win a bet on this kind of line, the chosen team has only to win the game, either if it is the favorite or the underdog; it does not matter by how many points. Example:

A) Seattle Seahawks -140 *(favorite team, and the visitor)*
Detroit Lions +120 *(underdog, and the home team)*

The number after a minus (-) always denotes how much must be risked to win $100 and the number next to the plus (+) sign, how much would be won in the case of risking $100. In other words, negative money lines risk more to win less and positive money lines risk less to win more.

B) Chicago Bears -115
New York Giants -105

In this case, since the bettor must risk slightly more $115, on the Bears, than on the Giants $105, to win $100, the Bears would be considered the *favorite*.

You can convert a moneyline to a decimal line. If the line is a negative number (favorite), divide 1 into the line making this one a two digit number the and add 1 to it.
Example:
-150 = 1 ÷ 1.50 = 0.8 +1 = 1.8
-120 = 1 ÷ 1.20 = 0.8333 +1 = 1.8333

If the line is a positive number (underdog), make it a two-digit number and just add 1 to it.
Example:
+150 = 1.50 + 1 = 2.5

Whenever the money line is EV (even money), which means +100, what you do is the same thing you do with a positive line, make it a 2 digit number (1.00) and add 1 to it, so the factor line would be 2.00.

FLAT LINE – This means that both lines on the two sides are -110 (or 10 percent juice).

POINTSPREAD (HANDICAP) – Amount of points that the team wagered on, has got to cover (win by more than or loose by less than), for the customer to win the wager. For example, when the bettor chooses the favorite team on the spread, the team must win by more than the points taken from it. If the New York Giants are listed –8 on the spread, they must win by more than 8 points; if the difference on the final score is exactly 8 points, the wager is a push (the money wagered on the team will be returned to the account). If they do not win by more than 8 points, the wager is a loss.

In case of choosing the underdog, the team can lose by less than the points given to it. If San Francisco 49'ers are +8, it means that the bettor can lose by less than 7 points or win outright; if the difference is exactly 8, the wager is a push (the money will be returned to the account). If they lose by more than 8, it is a loss.

PICK – This means there are no points to cover and the team just has to win the game, in order to be able to win a wager made on that line. Neither team is favored; take your pick and lay 11 to 10.

GAME TOTALS – A wager where the combined score of the two teams will exceed (the over) or be less than (the under) a certain number. Sometimes there can be a favorite, determined by the highest juice. In Football and Basketball there is a point spread to be covered, and the juice is usually –110 (10%), unless there is a special situation on the game and the juice changes. In all other sports, money lines will determine the risk and win.

FIXED ODDS – In fixed-odds bets, the odds are fixed at standard odds -110, or 10 percent juice ($110 bet winning $100). The fixed odds are set according to the chart below and only apply to football and basketball pointspreads or totals. All the picks must have standard odds. If any of the picks involve other sports, Moneylines, Buy Points or off-standard lines (-115, etc.), then the parlay becomes subject to True Odds.

TRUE ODDS – To calculate the true odds payoff,

simply convert the moneyline or odds to a multiplier (you can find the calculation table in the help section of most sports books), and then multiply your bet by the product of the multipliers. For example, if you make a $10 parlay on two picks with true odds of -140 converts to 1.71 and odds of +120 converts to 2.20. Therefore,

your payout is as follows: 10 x 1.71 x 2.20 = $37.62. Note that this payout includes your original wager, so the net win in this example would be $27.62.

For example: If the Pittsburgh Steelers are –5 and you buy two points to make the Steelers –3 (which is a key number), the line would change to –3 (-165) and you

EUROPEAN SOCCER BETTING AT BODOG SPORTSBOOK

All Times Eastern						
Select A Sport ▼	Single	Parlay	Teaser	Add to Picks	Update Lines	
Sat, Mar 12, 05		Spread	Moneyline	Total		Score
7:15a **English FA Cup**						Recap
8201 Bolton			+275 ☐		0 Final	
8202 Arsenal			-120 ☐		1	
8203 Draw			+220 ☐			

The score at the end of regulation (90 minutes + injury time) will be used for wagering purposes and does not include results from extra time, golden-goals or penalty shoot-outs.

12:15p **English FA Cup**						Preview
8203 Southampton			+450 ☐			
8204 Manchester United			-188 ☐			
8205 Draw			+250 ☐			

The score at the end of regulation (90 minutes + injury time) will be used for wagering purposes and does not include results from extra time, golden-goals or penalty shoot-outs.

10:00a **English League Championship**						In Progress
8215 Burnley FC			-164 ☐			
8216 Rotherdam United			+400 ☐			
8217 Draw			+230 ☐			
10:00a **English League Championship**						In Progress
8217 Coventry City			EVEN ☐			
8218 Cardiff City			+225 ☐			
8219 Draw			+225 ☐			
10:00a **English League Championship**						In Progress
8219 Crewe Alexandra			+300 ☐			
8220 Sunderland FC			-139 ☐			

Moneylines are displayed here as check boxes in the middle column. Bets are placed by clicking the appropriate check boxes and then submitting the bet.

NBA BASKETBALL LINES AT BODOG SPORTSBOOK

All Times Eastern					
Select A Sport ▼	Single	Parlay	Teaser	Add to Picks	Update Lines

Sat, Mar 12, 05		Spread	Moneyline	Total	Score
1:05p Game can be seen on YES				Matchup | Preview | Injuries	
501	New Jersey Nets	+10½ (-115) ☐	+425 ☐	190 Over ☐	
502	Miami Heat	-10½ (-105) ☐	-650 ☐	Under ☐	
7:05p Game can be seen on FOX-Bay , Turnersouth				Matchup | Preview | Injuries	
503	Golden State Warriors	-4 ☐		194 (-105)o ☐	
504	Atlanta Hawks	+4 ☐		(-115)u ☐	
7:05p				Matchup | Preview | Injuries	
505	Los Angeles Lakers	-6 (-115) ☐		194 Over ☐	
506	Charlotte Bobcats	+6 (-105) ☐		Under ☐	
8:05p				Matchup | Preview | Injuries	
507	Milwaukee Bucks	Pick ☐		185 Over ☐	
508	New Orleans Hornets	Pick ☐		Under ☐	
8:35p				Matchup | Preview | Injuries	
509	Denver Nuggets				
510	San Antonio Spurs				

A pointspread wager, as displayed at BoDog.com. Pointspread's are typically used for high-scoring sports like basketball and American football. Notice the Milwaukee/New Orleans game is listed as a "pick." This means that neither team is favored and that the team that is picked must win for the bet to pay off.

would have to pay $165 to win $100.

PARLAYS (ACCUMULATORS) – Also known as a "combo", is a selection of two or more wagering outcomes, in which the odds for the payouts increase with the number of teams (sides/totals) chosen; the more teams you choose the better the payout. You may combine different sports, pointspreads and moneylines in win/loss and/or totals betting. You may also buy points in betting a parlay (see Fig. A).

TEASER – A teaser is a selection of two or more outcomes in a single wager in which either the pointspread or total is adjusted in the bettor's favor. Each sport has its own range of points for teaser selections. A teaser adjusts the spread for the favorite so that it

Fig. A: PARLAY ODDS

# of Teams	Actual Odds	Las Vegas Payout	House Edge
2	3/1	2.6/1	10.0%
3	7/1	6/1	12.5%
4	15/1	10/1	31.25%
5	31/1	20/1	34.38%
6	63/1	40/1	35.94%
7	127/1	75/1	40.63%
8	255/1	150/1	41.02%
9	511/1	300/1	41.21%
10	1027/1	700/1	31.54%

ARENA FOOTBALL BETTING AT BODOG SPORTSBOOK

All Times Eastern					
Select A Sport ▾	Single	Parlay	Teaser	Add to Picks	Update Lines

Sat, Mar 12, 05		Spread		Total	Score
7:00p				Matchup	Preview	Injuries	
453	Georgia Force	+5½ ☐	100	Over ☐	
454	New York Dragons	-5½ ☐		Under ☐	
7:00p				Matchup	Preview	Injuries	
455	Las Vegas Gladiators	-5 ☐	96	Over ☐	
456	Columbus Destroyers	+5 ☐		Under ☐	
8:30p				Matchup	Preview	Injuries	
457	Colorado Crush	-8 ☐	97	Over ☐	
458	Nashville Kats	+8 ☐		Under ☐	

Betting totals, displayed here in the right column, is another popular betting option for high-scoring sports.

decreases the posted spread, or conversely, increases the posted spread for the underdog. If you select a total, the adjustment makes totals higher-to-go-under or lower-to-go-over. All the picks must win, if one loses the entire wager is a loss. If one pick is a push the teaser reverts to the next lower number of picks.

SWEETHEART TEASER – Is a special teaser for either basketball or football where you can choose between 3 or 4 picks (sides/totals) instead of the regular points, you may tease football by 10 (3 sides/totals) and 13 (4 sides/totals) points and basketball by 8 (3 team) and 10 (4 team) points. A push in a sweetheart teaser is a loss. Sweetheart teasers never reduce. There are no sweetheart teasers for baseball. If one pick is a push, the wager is automatically a loss also.

ROUND ROBIN – A series of three or more teams into two-team wagers. When you choose multiple picks and then combine them into a series of parlays. For example, you may choose three teams and then want to round robin them into three or two team parlays.

FUTURE BETS – Future bets are odds posted in advance, on the winners of various major events including: Super Bowl, the World Series, the Stanley Cup, the NBA Championship. These odds can be posted a few days in advance or up to several months ahead of the event time. On wagers such as the winner of the next Super Bowl, all bets have to be placed before the start of the official season. As soon as the first game of the regular season starts the lines are taken off the board.

PROPOSITION BETS – A prop or proposition bet is a wager with 2 or more outcomes that is not directly related to the final score of an event; they are also called "exotics." Most featured props are single bets only (cannot be parlayed). For example, a bet on how many yards Payton Manning will throw in his next game: less than 100; 101-150; 151-200; 201-250; 251-300 or 300+. There will be posted odds for each outcome.

A common entry in prop bets is a field entry. This is a catch-all category for any competitor not specifically listed in the prop, but is competing in the event. For example, a prop on a PGA event might list odds for the best 30 players: Tiger Woods 1/1, David Duval 5/1, etc. As PGA events often have 75 or more competitors, the other 45+ players that do not have odds posted individually would be listed indirectly as past of the field. If any of the players in the field win, the field would be declared the winner for wagering purposes.

IF BETS – An if bet, like a parlay, allows you to link together two or more individual bets. Unlike a parlay, it is not an all or nothing bet. You are essentially instructing the sports book that "if" the first bet wins, then place a second bet on this other proposition. If your first bet wins, the sports book will place your second bet. If your first bet loses, there will be no second bet. This type of bet is primarily used as a form of money management.

REVERSES – These are simply 2 to 8 straight bets joined together into if bets that work in both directions of the if clause, the risk is the same for all the wagers in the reversal; buying points is allowed. If one pick is a push, the wager is automatically a loss. The more teams selected in the reverse, the more possible combinations there will be and the higher amount of money that must be risked.

Searching for the Right Sports Book

Now that you know what you're looking for in an online sports book, where do you start your search? Here's a step-by-step approach:

- ● DO YOUR RESEARCH. Before you sign up with any sports book, it is always good to do a bit of online research. Read recent reviews in industry magazines, visit a few forums to see what other bettors are saying. If a book hasn't been around a few years, how do you know they have the resources to survive a tough week, month or season? That's not to say that all new books are bad, just that you may have to dig deeper before you trust them with your money.

FOOTBALL FUTURES BETTING AT BODOG SPORTSBOOK

All Times Eastern

Select A Sport ▼	Single	Parlay	Teaser	Add to Picks	Update Lines

These events are only available for wagering via the Internet

Odds to win 2006 Super Bowl	Odds
All wagers have Action. No Parlays	
	Preview
Arizona Cardinals	90/1 ☐
Atlanta Falcons	18/1 ☐
Baltimore Ravens	18/1 ☐
Buffalo Bills	22/1 ☐
Carolina Panthers	25/1 ☐
Chicago Bears	48/1 ☐
Cincinnati Bengals	38/1 ☐
Cleveland Browns	170/1 ☐
Dallas Cowboys	40/1 ☐
Denver Broncos	28/1 ☐
Detroit Lions	38/1 ☐
Green Bay Packers	30/1 ☐
Houston Texans	55/1 ☐

Football futures betting at Bodog Sportsbook: The Super Bowl is one of the most popular futures bets. It often attracts casual bettors and sports fanatics.

⚫ DETERMINE WHETHER THE SPORTS BOOK SUITS YOUR NEEDS. Once you've selected a few sports books, check to see that they've got everything you're looking for. Weed out those that don't.

⚫ CALL THEIR CUSTOMER SERVICE LINE. Does it even offer 24-hour customer service? With your money on the line, you will want to test their customer service by asking a variety of questions. If you've got any concerns at all, this is where you'll want to get some answers.

Helpful Tips to Get You Started

If you do nothing else, here are a couple of helpful tips to keep in mind before you place your bets:

OPEN MORE THAN ONE ACCOUNT – If you have an account at only one sports book, you have no choice but to either accept the line offered or not bet. If you use two sports books, you can compare the lines you get and wager on the one that provides you with the best opportunity to win your bet. It's up to you to decide how many books you should use. Too few means you don't have enough variation in the lines, but if you have too many, you may lose some opportunities as it will take too long to shop all the lines and your bankroll could be spread too thin. Be sure to choose sports books where it is easy to get the lines you need very quickly. The magic number is probably somewhere between three and five books for most people, but if you only have one account, even getting two more sets of lines to look at for every game should make a big difference to your bottom line at the end of the season. Getting a few extra wins or pushes over the course of the season makes that extra shopping well worth the effort.

SHOP FOR THE BEST LINES POSSIBLE – Pros use a couple of guidelines for shopping football lines. Generally the public prefers favorites and over with the total so the lines tend to move in that direction (but not all the time or books would simply raise those opening lines). Thus, the rule-of-thumb is to play favorites and overs early and to play underdogs and unders late. You won't get the best line every time following this rule, but it should serve as a solid base and will boost your win percentage.

GOOD MONEY MANAGEMENT – Money is an emotional thing. The more you have, the more you spend. If you

don't have enough of it, then you're left wanting more. Generally speaking, those two factors alone will drive people to do things that they probably shouldn't do. To avoid heading down this path, however, here's what you should do: Keep your bets to reasonable, affordable and consistent amounts and your bankroll will last a long time. If you can pick more than 52.4 percent winners, you will come out ahead of the book in the long run and that is the only time frame that matters.

STICK TO SPORTS YOU KNOW. There's an old joke in the industry about the guy who ran his account balance right down to the ground. He went 0-5 on baseball for the day, 0-5 on basketball for the day, and 0-5 on football for the day. So one night he calls the book manager, desperate to get something back. He asks the book manager, "What else have you got on the boards?" The book manager says, "Well, baseball's done, basketball's done, football's done, but I do have a late hockey game." So the guy says, "Hockey? What do I know about hockey?" To which the book manager replies, "Look, you're 0-15 for the day. What do you know about football, basketball, or baseball?"

When it comes to how do your money management skills stack up? Ask yourself the following questions:

⚫ After a short-term winning period, are you quick to raise your bet amounts for the following week?
⚫ After a short-term losing period, do you then lower the amount of your plays?
⚫ Do you (or have you ever) put all of your action on one game?
⚫ Do you ever find yourself chasing your losses?

If you answered "yes" to any or all of those questions, you may want to consider breaking a bad habit (or two). Poor money management generates more losses for players than bad handicapping. Even the worst bettors seldom lose more than 55% of their picks. On the other hand, good money management skills will not always make you a winner (that still has to come from choosing the right teams), but it will help your bankroll last.

Whatever sport is your passion, knowing that you can safely place your wagers online can only add to the overall experience. Watch with your heart and bet with your head.

BETTING EXCHANGES

For an increasing band of punters, a Gloucestershire, England farmhouse holds as much significance as a Bethlehem stable does to a churchgoer.

Because it was as he sat in his West Country cottage in one of his moments of naturally blurred boredom and brilliance that Andrew Black hit upon the idea of Betfair. What followed in the next six years has literally transformed the face of betting worldwide, as Black, in conjunction with his company's co-founder, Edward Wray, developed a product that would revolutionize wagering.

The idea was simple, yet staggering. Partial to a punt himself, and fed up with the limited prices and service that the traditional bookmakers were offering, Black looked at the New York stock exchange and immediately saw a massive hole in the UK's traditional bookmaking model.

Black's spark of genius was to match the model to betting on sport and horseracing, and it resulted in the advent of betting exchanges.

What is the betting exchange concept and why is it so popular?

Betting exchanges let their punters choose their odds; they enable punters set their own prices rather than accept whatever is set by the operator of the service (as would be true with a traditional bookmaker). All bets on an exchange are placed by users who either want bet that something will happen (also known as backing) or bet that it won't happen (also known as laying). Bets are matched between people with opposing views.

How are betting exchanges different from conventional bookmakers?

- Exchanges let you bet that something will or won't happen.
- Exchanges let you choose the odds.
- Because of the efficiencies of the betting exchange model, punters can expect odds that average up to 20 percent better on exchanges. Punters then only have to pay a small commission on their net winnings on any event to the exchange, with the commission set according to the market. There is no commission on losing wagers.

- Betting exchanges let you bet whilst the game is in play (also known as betting "in-running"). Some consider this to be the biggest attraction of betting exchanges.
- Winners are always welcome at exchanges as are all bet sizes (providing there are people with a counter view).

"With the FTSE there are a lot of brokers who just put their prices up. In New York you ring your broker and say 'I want to buy,' and he'll go and just stick your bid on the board. Anyone can come and post their bid on the board, which creates a great big matching system. There is almost a beauty to a really efficient industry."

— *Andrew Black, Founder, Betfair*

The Fundamental Difference

In some respects, betting exchanges provide a peer-to-peer platform that on the face of it looks not unlike that of eBay. Because the exchanges use sophisticated bookmaking technology to balance their books perfectly, the effect (though not the fact) is that the participants bet against each other at a price which reflects true market value. When using a traditional sports book, on the other hand, the bookie balances his book as best he can as he takes bets from different punters, and to account for his added risk, he adds an extra fee into his price.

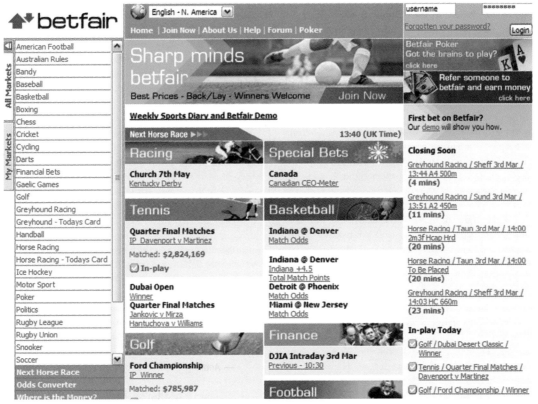

Betfair.com is the world's largest and oldest online betting exchange.

BACK OR LAY – When you "back" a selection (be it an individual, a team, horse, dog or other), you are betting that it will win. When you "lay" it, you are betting against it winning. For example, if you're betting in a market on which team is going to win the English Soccer Premiership and you lay Manchester United, you offer odds to other punters who wish to back United. If United doesn't win, then you pick up the backer's stake. If United wins, then you pay out.

Although the exchange knows all the details of each bet and the source of funds behind it, the customer never knows who he or she is betting against. Therefore, provided it is a secure site, the privacy and confidentiality of all customers' bets are maintained.

CHOOSE ODDS – With betting exchanges, there is always a choice of what odds to accept. If you want better odds than what's available, you can place an order for a better price. But be realistic because there has to be somebody prepared to take the bet at those odds, and vice versa.

Take a look at the odds before a game and you will see them change as visitors back and lay their bets. The odds often improve nearer to the off, as there are more people in the market.

BETTER ODDS AND COMMISSION – Commission is only paid on your net winnings on each market. This is particularly beneficial if you have multiple bets on a single market, such as the Premiership Winner market. Some of your bets may win, and some may lose, but you only pay commission on your net winnings. If your bets in a particular market amount to a net loss, you do not pay commission.

It is of course true to say that betting exchanges charge winning punters—unlike the high street bookmakers—but that charge is more than offset by the odds that are available. Short-priced horses may only be available at 5 to 10% better odds on a betting exchange, but for outsiders, it is regularly 100 percent (or more) better on exchanges. All leading exchanges offer a customer incentive scheme.

BETTING 'IN-PLAY' OR 'IN-RUNNING' – Ask a betting exchange user what he likes most about the product, and I'll wager most will say betting in-running. When the tapes go up in the Grand National (horse race), for example, that spells the end of the betting with the traditional bookmakers. But on an exchange you can bet right up until the first horse passes the winning line some nine minutes later. This is true in all live sporting events: You can bet up until the result is officially known.

Betting in-running also enables punters to take a profit, or have a no-risk bet, if their pre-event prediction is proven correct in the early stages. Take this scenario in a football (soccer) match, for example:

If that bets gets taken, the original backer of Liverpool at 2-1 would be in the enviable situation of winning $100 is if Liverpool win, but losing nothing should they fail to hold on to their lead. The backer can simply sit back and enjoy the rest of the game, safe in the knowledge he can only win.

Perhaps the most exciting feature offered at betting exchanges, in-running bets allow the punter to wager on an event as it is taking place. The checkmark icon is displayed next to all in-running bets.

WINNERS ARE WELCOME – We have all heard tales of shrewd and winning customers having their accounts closed by disgruntled bookmakers, and many of us have experienced getting our intended $50 bet at 25-1 refused and reduced accordingly. The advantage of betting exchanges is that they match up all the risk between different sets of opposing punters, so they know that every bet makes them money. As a result, they have no direct interest in the outcome of any event, so they won't close you down or restrict your stake size.

Answering the Inevitable Questions

The concept of person-to-person betting inevitably raises questions in people's minds: How can I be sure I get paid? How do I know that someone isn't fleecing me, knowing more than I do (and effectively trading on inside information)? And isn't there a worry that people will start to rig events if they can bet on outcomes not happening?

Of course, if those questions had not been answered by the exchanges themselves when the concept was launched, they would never have had the success that they have in such a short period. Ultimately, if there's real doubt surrounding the integrity of the product, people won't use it—and millions of bets going through every day give the lie to that.

The payment side is the simplest to address: Every bet is fully collateralised, which means that you have to put your entire liability up front. The system is intelligent, in that $100 can be used for more than one bet, providing your risk is not increased. So, you can oppose one horse for $10 at 10/1, and another in the same race in $20 at 5/1, on the basis that your worst case scenario is that the 5/1 shot runs in (liability $100), whereupon you pick up the $10 stake on the other.

The question of inside information has been addressed as well (and not just with the thought that there's never anyone more inside than a bookmaker because it's his job to make sure he knows more about an event than you do). Exchanges minimize the chances of people misusing information by reaching information-sharing agreements with sporting bodies to ensure that the rules of the game are upheld.

Under those agreements—or Memoranda of Understanding, as they are known—exchanges can pass on information relating to the bets of their clients to the administrative body of the sport in question, if it is suspected that the rules of that sport have been broken. It is a condition of using the exchange that you agree for that information to be given up. With their sophisticated audit trail, which tracks and records every detail of every bet (and the deposit and withdrawal of every penny to keep a complete handle on source of funds), the capability of policing is significantly improved, and its effect has been welcomed by sporting bodies across the world.

This also addresses the third issue—that of someone trying to rig an event. While it is argued that exchanges allow people to rig events, it is also argued that agreements with sports bodies actual increase the ability to detect corruption by creating by creating a clear and transparent audit trail through which suspicious betting activity can be monitored. And while betting exchanges may have simplified the mechanism by which you can bet on an outcome not happening, they have not increased the number of people who are connected with the sporting event in question, who have always been able to bet teams and horses to lose in any case. It can be argued that by clarifying the process of placing the bets, exchanges have increased the ability to police it. The bottom line on corruption: Wherever there is a chance to make money, there will be someone who tries to take advantage of the system. Throughout the history of sport, making money from an outcome not happening has been through a rudimentary understanding of mathematics, friendly bookmakers, or the spread betting markets. In other words, try corrupting sport on an exchange, and it's very short odds that you're going to get caught.

A Simple Guide to Exchange Betting

THE BASIC CONCEPT—The prerequisite of placing your funds and bets in the hands of any bookmaker is complete confidence in them.

A model for safe-guarding funds has been adopted as standard across the industry, and as part of the betting exchange "Code of Conduct" agreed with by the government, all UK betting exchanges are obliged to ring-fence deposited funds in a separate account. Sites that abide by the code only release funds once a bet is settled.

Once you are happy with the exchange you have chosen, it is time to make the product work for you. In that respect, it is also essential that a betting exchange has plenty of liquidity (i.e. plenty of money to both back and lay) so punters can change their positions if they so wish. The problem with some of the smaller exchanges is that there is simply no money of real note in the markets. This is an important consideration to make before choosing an exchange. The best advice is to monitor the exchange for a couple of days prior to making a deposit.

Newcastle v Tottenham - Match Odds | Refresh

☑ View P&L [Settings] ?   102.3% 99.5%

Total selections:(3) USD			Back	Lay		
Newcastle	1.98 $141	2.04 $190	2.06 $53	2.08 $9	2.1 $78	2.12 $9
Tottenham	3.6 $50	4 $171	4.1 $42	4.3 $290	4.4 $10	5 $19
The Draw	3.25 $696	3.35 $178	3.4 $67	3.55 $88	3.6 $27	

Weekend English FA Cup

Betfair expresses its odds in decimal terms. To find out how much your bet pays, multiply the bet by the decimal number. In this example, a winning $100 bet placed on Newcastle would translate to a $206 payout (a $106 profit) for the backer. Expressed fractionally, the odds would be 53/50, or slightly more than even money (2.0).

Below is a basic run-through of how you go about placing a bet on an exchange. Some flesh can be added to those bare bones a little later. We have used Betfair as an example in this instance because it offers punters some extra, interesting, easy-to-use features.

IT MAY LOOK DIFFERENT, BUT IT DOESN'T TAKE LONG TO MASTER – Betting exchanges do not use traditional odds such as 11-8, 13-2, etc. Instead the odds are expressed in decimal terms. Just as when betting at Tote odds on a horse race, the odds include the one-unit stake that is returned with the winnings. For example, if you back Arsenal at odds of 2.3 for $100, you want Arsenal to win. Your total return if they do win will be $230 (including your stake), and your loss if they don't is $100 (your stake). Exchanges charge a small commission on the net winnings, which is stated up front and is dependent on your turnover. No commission is charged on losing bets.

Fractional	Decimal	American
10/1	11	$1,000.00
9/1	10	$900.00
8/1	9	$800.00
15/2	8.5	$750.00
7/1	8	$700.00
13/2	7.5	$650.00
6/1	7	$600.00
11/2	6.5	$550.00
5/1	6	$500.00
9/2	5.5	$450.00
4/1	5	$400.00
7/2	4.5	$350.00
3/1	4	$300.00
5/2	3.5	$250.00
2/1	3	$200.00
7/4	2.75	$175.00
7/5	2.4	$140.00
5/4	2.25	$125.00
6/5	2.2	$120.00
1/1	2	($100.00)
9/10	1.9	($111.10)
5/6	1.833	($120.00)
4/5	1.8	($125.00)
8/11	1.727	($137.50)
7/10	1.7	($142.90)

This table displays conversions of common fractional odds to the decimal odds system used by Betfair.com.

TAKING THE ODDS AVAILABLE – Having decided what you think will happen in the game, and what you want to do as a result, you hit the relevant price on the screen. Depending on which outcome you are choosing, the best price is shown either in blue or in pink.

Orlando @ Cleveland - Match Odds							Refresh
☑ View P&L [Settings] [?]			100.4%	97.8%			
Total selections:(2)	USD		Back	Lay			
Orlando Magic	3.25 $345	3.4 $2909	3.45 $1894	3.65 $105	3.7 $22	3.75 $13	
Cleveland Cavaliers	1.38 $16	1.39 $65	1.4 $102	1.42 $582	1.43 $133	1.45 $11	

Betfair highlights the best prices in blue (back) and pink (lay).

If you're happy with the odds on offer at Betfair, you press the "submit" button. In the same example, you had $100 at 2.3 on Arsenal which, if successful, would return $230 ($130 winnings plus the $100 stake) before commission.

REQUESTING BETTER ODDS – If you want better odds—such as $100 at 2.34 on Arsenal—simply change the "Your Odds" box with the up and down arrows, and press submit. Your bet then appears as an offer in the lay column. Unmatched bets are matched on the basis of best-price-first, and then on a first-come first-served basis.

STATUS OF YOUR BETS ONCE INPUT—A bet can have the following statuses:

- ⚬ MATCHED BETS are those that have been successfully placed.
- ⚬ UNMATCHED BETS are those that have been placed, but have yet to be matched by other users. These bets can be cancelled.
- ⚬ LAPSED BETS are unmatched bets that have been cancelled when a market has closed.
- ⚬ VOIDED BETS are matched bets that have been cancelled due to a change in market conditions, such as your selection in a horse race being declared a non runner.
- ⚬ CANCELLED BETS are those that are removed by customers before they are matched.

Further Important Features of Betfair

PROFIT AND LOSS – Clicking the "View P&L" tick box on the top left corner of the odds table displays the user's profit (in green) or loss (in red) should each selection win or lose.

ACCOUNT DETAILS – The "My Account" button brings up a number of options:

- CURRENT BETS lists all unsettled bets.
- BETTING HISTORY brings up an easy summary of all bets, which can be categorised into events and downloaded to a spreadsheet.
- ACCOUNT FUNDS is used to deposit or withdraw money or to check your balance and liabilities.
- ACCOUNT STATEMENT brings up a comprehensive bank-type statement of all transactions.
- Profile lists your personal details registered with Betfair, which can be amended.

DIGGING DEEPER TO UNEARTH A POTENTIAL GOLDMINE – Betting exchanges may offer greater odds, value, control and choice, but they will certainly not turn you into a winning punter overnight. If you are a losing punter on any betting platform, you have to change your betting habits to turn the tide.

Ask any winning punter the pre-requisites of making money, and all should certainly include the three basic principles listed overleaf:

Unlike traditional sports books, betting exchanges allow you to pick your own odds, which can be adjusted by clicking the up and down arrows.

Divisional Winners 05 - AL East

View P&L [Settings] [?]   366.2% 65.2%

Total selections: (5)   USD

		Back	Lay		
New York Yankees		1.25 $38	1.59 $5	1.6 $11	1.8 $96
Boston Red Sox		1.1 $50	50 $5		
Baltimore Orioles	7.2 $50	7.4 $47	1000 $5		
Toronto Blue Jays		1.1 $50	1000 $5		
Tampa Bay Devil Rays		1.1 $50	1000 $5		

After picking your own odds at Betfair, the odds are displayed on the betting menu for everyone to see. No wager is placed, however, until at least one willing party takes the other side of the bet.

Current Bets (Unsettled Selections) - Demo Account 14-Mar-2005 14:48

Bet status: Unmatched ▼   Order by: ● Placed Date ○ Market

Showing 1 – 1 of 1 bets

Market	Selection	Type	Bet ID	Bet placed	Odds req.	Stake (£)	Cancel ?
0 UK / Taun 14th Mar / 14:50 2m Beg Chs	Andreas	Back	972662531	14-Mar-05 14:48	2	20.00	☐

Betfair makes it easy to monitor the status of your bets.

- Do your homework.
- Keep your discipline. (Don't become overconfident on a winning run or too downcast in a losing spell.)
- Most importantly, never bet more than you can afford or are willing to lose.

Making Exchanges Work for You

Punters have a head start on exchanges simply because exchanges offer better odds. If anything, you should at least hang on to your money longer before it disappears! But a head start is all it is: Bettors still have to approach, and reap the benefits of, exchanges in a variety of ways. While gamblers might benefit simply on account of the better odds available, arguably the most successful group of bettors on exchanges are what are known as the "traders."

GUARANTEEING A PROFIT BEFORE THE EVENT EVEN STARTS – Some traders successfully forecast the way the betting will move in any given market and bet accordingly. It's a similar skill to buying and selling shares profitably. But instead of buying low and selling high, exchange punters try to back high and lay low.

This has led to a familiar cry in exchange circles: "Don't tip me a winner, tip me the price." If you think you know what price a horse is going to start then you can attempt to trade yourself into a winning position before the race goes off. Be careful though: If the market turns against you, then you could be left with a book where all eventualities lose you money.

THE IN-RUNNING BETTORS AND TRADERS – Betting in-running is probably the number one attraction of exchanges, and in-running betting on horseracing is particularly fascinating. The one stipulation is that to make it pay, you need liquidity.

Punters have adopted a number of money-making strategies. One of the more commonly-used strategies is heavily backing a known frontrunner before the race and looking to lay it at a much lower price after it has (hopefully!) built up a big lead soon after the start.

Some people make this strategy pay, but there is no real magic rule. In fact, it's probably true that the more people use the strategy, the less effective it becomes. Whether you back a horse to lay it or lay it to back it—or whether you look for a lagging horse in-running and back it for a late spurt, or lay a front-runner you don't think will respond if pushed to the wire—there is a lot of luck in gambling. Being in the right place at the right time is not to be underestimated.

IN-RUNNING TALES FROM BETFAIR – In-running betting throws up some wonderful stories. AC Milan's 3–2 win over Sampdoria late in 2004 is one of the best. The pre-match odds-on favourites won it, which might come as no surprise. But the fact that they were down 2–0 as the match moved into the 88th minute changes the picture a little. One punter laid £1 at the magical maximum 1,000 on Milan—betting £999 that they would lose, and standing to win only £1 if he turned out to be right and they did. Of course, the comeback proved expensive for him. Another was betting at 1.05 that the match would end in a draw, as the match stood at 2–2 in the fourth minute of injury time (staking £20 to win £1). It's not for the faint-hearted!

But the punter who gets it right can laugh all the way to the bank. One took home £16,983 for £17 on Tony McCoy's mount Mini Sensation in a 4m Marathon handicap chase at Exeter in December 2004—again at the amazing odds of 1,000. Evidently, McCoy's ride to the halfway point hadn't impressed someone.

Ups and downs. Mini Sensation (above) earned one punter more than £16,000 from a £17 stake, and Internazionale of Milan (below) caused problems for bettors when they came from 2–0 behind to win a match 3–2 in the dying seconds.

HORSE RACING

Experience all the thrills of a day at
the track from your very own
comfortable armchair.

HORSE RACING

"In 1938, a year of monumental turmoil, the number-one newsmaker wasn't Franklin Roosevelt or Adolf Hitler. It wasn't even a person. It was an undersized, crooked-legged racehorse owned by a bicycle repairman turned automobile magnate, trained by a virtually mute mustang breaker, and ridden by a half-blind failed prizefighter. That racehorse was Seabiscuit." — *Seabiscuit*, by Laura Hillenbrand (2001)

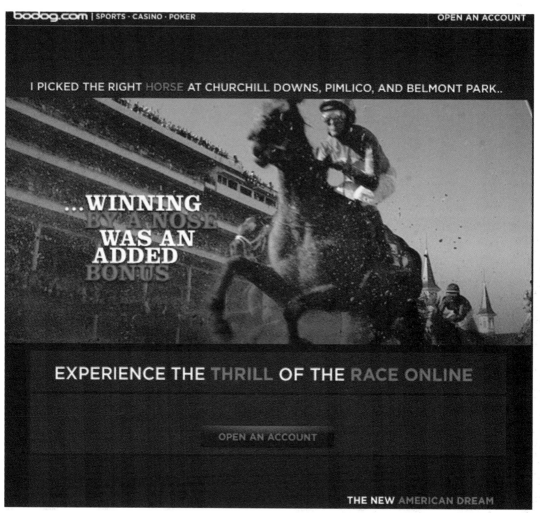

Welcome to the world of Internet race wagering.

In a time where war and politics made life increasingly difficult for most, horse racing gave people something to cheer about. For his final race on March 2, 1940 at Santa Anita, Seabiscuit drew a crowd of 78,000, which is the equivalent to a modern day Super Bowl crowd. Of course, there were other horses after Seabiscuit that would achieve greater fame and fortune, but by then horse racing had made a name for itself. Horse racing is now the second most widely attended U.S. spectator sport, after baseball, and is one of the most globally wagered upon of all professional sports.

Horse racing in the UK and Europe, horse racing in the US

Horse racing today exists primarily for gambling, but it is a major professional sport in the UK, Canada, Europe, Australia, New Zealand, South Africa and South America. With over five million people visiting British racecourses each year and a large television audience, horseracing is UK's second largest spectator sport after soccer.

While horse racing's popularity is universal, there are a number of differences that make racing in Europe different to horse racing in the United States (and vice versa):

DIFFERENT TRACKS: In the US, the tracks are oval-shaped, flat, dirt-surfaced, and about a mile around. Grass courses tend to be smaller, tighter, and tucked inside the main track. Belmont's mile-and-a-half, Woodbine's "outside" turf course, Kentucky Downs' pear-shape, and Santa Anita's hillside are exceptions. Courses in Europe come in all shapes and sizes, though most of the races are run on grass. Dirt surfaces are rare. Different Racing Seasons: In the US, race meetings are long, typically two to four months, and racing is held five or six days a week. The circuits are widely separated across the country, and racing starts on January 1 and "ends" on December 31. In Europe, race meetings are short. One-day meetings are the most common, and even the highly prestigious, like Royal Ascot or Glorious Goodwood, take place over five days at most. The European racing calendar is limited. Major "flat racing" starts in late March in England and Ireland, a bit earlier in France, and is over by the middle of November.

DIFFERENT CROWDS: If you were to ask a European, they would tell you that the horse racing crowds in Europe are bigger, and its spectators are well-dressed.

For many Europeans, going to the races is an occasion.

TRADITION: The oldest English horse races are the longest-running sporting events in the world.

HORSE RACES WORLDWIDE:
- Hong Kong Cup: The international invitational at Sha Tin in Hong Kong.
- Japan Cup: The international invitational in Tokyo.
- Melbourne Cup: The biggest race in Australia.
- Prix de l'Arc de Triomphe: The biggest race in Europe held at Longchamp in Paris.
- Royal Ascot: England's premier race meet of the year.
- The Grand National: The Aintree Martell Grand National.
- Queen's Plate: Canada's big race for 3-year-old Canadian thoroughbreds.

American Thoroughbred Racing

Although the sport became a popular local pastime, the development of organized horse racing did not arrive until after the Civil War. With the rapid rise of an industrial economy, gambling on racehorses, and therefore horse racing itself, grew explosively; by 1890, 314 tracks were operating across the country. In 1894 the nation's most prominent track and stable owners formed the American Jockey Club.

The sport prospered until World War II, declined in popularity during the 1950s and 1960s, then enjoyed a resurgence in the 1970s triggered by the immense popularity of great horses such as Secretariat, Seattle Slew and Affirmed, each winners of the American Triple Crown – the Kentucky Derby, the Preakness, and the Belmont Stakes.

Today, much of the focus is primarily on major thoroughbred races such as the American Triple Crown and the Breeders' Cup races.

THE TRIPLE CROWN is the Kentucky Derby: 1¼ Miles (Churchill Downs—First Saturday in May); Preakness Stakes: 1³⁄₁₆ Miles (Pimilco Race Course—Third Saturday in May); Belmont Stakes: 1½ Miles (Belmont Stakes— Three Weeks After Preakness).

From course to computer

Technology has taken the action of the live tracks, brought it to the World Wide Web, and has made it possible for anyone with a computer to wager on practically any race online. If you want to place your wagers at any North American online racetrack you have several options to choose from:

OPEN AN ACCOUNT with a North American based online racebook and wager into the official pari-mutuel pools just as if they were at the racetrack. When wagering with these types of companies you have the same advantages and disadvantages to placing your wagers at the track or an OTB (Off-Track Betting Location). These wagers are a part of the same pools that determine the payouts. This means large wagers can affect the final odds and the amount of money that the wagers pay. Large wins are subject to the state and federal regulations concerning taxes. There are no maximum wagers and no maximum payouts, as the racebook assumes no risk on wagers. All wagers are subject to the rules and regulations of the track the wagers were placed on concerning refunds, cancellations, etc. These racebooks are accepting wagers in cooperation with the host tracks and therefore most offer live video and audio feed to their players so you can listen and watch the race from your computer. Examples include TVG.com and youbet.com

OPEN AN ACCOUNT with an offshore online racebook and wager outside of the pari-mutuel pools. Some players prefer to wager offshore because of concern over taxes or a preference to wager without affecting the odds. Also, offshore racebooks commonly offer rebates based on different forms of player handle. The disadvantages are maximum wager amounts and maximum payouts as an offshore racebook assumes full risk on wagers. Examples include Bodog.com and Ehorse.com

OPEN AN ACCOUNT with an online betting exchange (popular in the UK). These books offer a completely different wagering option for players. Basically, you become your own bookie and can post or accept odds for or against a horse to win. You'll have to research this one a little more as it can get rather complicated to explain. (Visit ehorse.com for a tutorial on how to wager with an online betting exchange.) Examples are ehorseX and the widely popular Betfair.com.

What makes for a great racebook?

That depends. If you are interested in placing your online wagers within one the official pari-mutuel pools, then you should look for a site that offers most or all of the tracks you wish to wager on and access to live video. If you are looking for a site that falls into the second option (outside of the pari-mutuel pools) you should look for a site that offers high rebates based on total handle vs. losses, or other variables that are sometimes used.

Other betting advantages to keep in mind: high deposit bonuses, high maximums on wagers, and high maximums on payouts as well as the usual. Placing your wagers with an online betting exchange is still relatively new to North American players and North American racebooks, and therefore there are not as many exchange options available. As with any online gambling site, in the end it comes down to making sure that all of those essential, key ingredients – easy to use software, good customer service, variety of wagering options – are also in place.

Why Wager Online?

There's nothing quite like being at the racetrack. Placing your wagers at the ticket window and then watching your horse win by a nose is truly exciting, but the Internet makes it possible for you to place your wagers at any number of racetracks, from around the world. After placing your wagers online, you can then watch the race on television. All from the comfort of your own home.

The Different Types of Wager

PARI-MUTUEL WAGERING – A form of wagering that originated in France. When you place your wager at the track, that money goes into a betting pool. Each type of wager has its own betting pool. The track, serving as an agent or broker, receives a commission or "takeout" for handling the wagers.

STRAIGHT WAGERS – Straight wagers are single wagers that are placed on one horse.

WIN – You collect only if your horse finishes first. The minimum wager is $2.

PLACE – You collect only if your horse finishes first or second. You collect only the place amount. The minimum wager is $2.

SHOW – You collect only if your horse finishes first, second, or third. You collect only the show amount. The

Before you place your wagers, it's always a good idea to read up on the essential how-to steps.

minimum wager is $2.

ACROSS THE BOARD – A common term for placing all three straight wagers on one horse. You collect the win, place and show amount if your horse finishes first. You collect the place and show amount if your horse finishes second. You collect only the show amount if your horse finishes third. The minimum wager is $2 and would result in a total cost of $6 for the three straight wagers.

EXOTIC WAGERS – Exotic or combination wagers are wagers that involve two or more horses. The availability of these wagers varies depending on the race. It is always best to confirm in the program what exotic wagers are available before handicapping.

EXACTA (STRAIGHT FORECASTS) – To collect you must select the horses that finish first and second in exact order. For example, if you place a 3-5 exacta wager, the #3 horse must finish first and the #5 horse must finish second in order for you to collect. The minimum wager is $2.

TRIFECTA – To collect you must select the horses that finish first, second and third in exact order. This is similar to an exacta, only more difficult to handicap and therefore will usually pay more. The minimum wager is $2.

SUPERFECTA – To collect you must select the horses that finish first, second, third and fourth in exact order. Also similar to an exactor and trifecta, this wager is very difficult to handicap but will often pay even more than the trifecta. The minimum wager is $2.

The exacta, trifecta and superfecta wagers can also be boxed. When you box your wager you are extending your wager to include any finishing order containing only your selections. For example, if you place a 3-5 exacta box, the #3 horse may finish first and the #5 horse may finish second or the #5 horse may finish first and the #3 horse may finish second in order for you to collect. When you box you are actually placing multiple wagers and must pay for each possible combination your wager covers. The minimum wager when boxing is $1, but the total cost will depend on the number of horses you have selected. For example, the 3-5 exacta box with two possible outcomes to collect, if placed for $2 would come to a total cost of $4.

DAILY DOUBLE – To collect you must select the winner of two consecutive races. You must select your horses and place your wager before the first of the two races. The minimum wager is $2 when selecting one horse in each race.

PICK 3 – Similar to the daily double, to collect you must select the winner of three consecutive races. You must place your wager before the first of the three races. The minimum wager is $1 when selecting one horse in each race.

PICK 4 – Similar to the daily double and Win 3, to collect you must select the winner of four consecutive races. You must place your wager before the first of the four races. The minimum wager is $1 when selecting one horse in each race.

You can select more than one horse in some or all of the races when placing a daily double, pick 3 or pick 4. The minimum wager when making multiple selections is $1 for the daily double as well. To calculate the cost of your wager you would multiply the number of selections in the first race of the wager by the number of selections in subsequent races.

Calculating the Cost of Exotic Wagers

Simple formulae can help you compute the cost of your exotic wagers so you know what you are spending before you place your wager:

EXACTA BOX FORMULA: Number of selections x next lowest number x amount of wager
· Example:
$2 Exactor Box 3-5-7: 3 x 2 x 2 = $12
TRIFECTA BOX FORMULA: Number of selections x next

lowest number x next lowest number x amount of wager

Example:

$1 Triactor Box 3-5-7: 3 x 2 x 1 x 1 = $6

SUPERFECTA BOX FORMULA: Number of selections x next lowest number x next lowest number x next lowest number x amount of wager

Example:

$2 Superfecta Box 3-5-7-9: 4 x 3 x 2 x 1 x 2 = $48

DAILY DOUBLE, PICK 3 AND PICK 4 FORMULA: Number of selections in first race x number of selections in next race (continued for number of races) x amount of wager

Example:

$1 Win 3 2,4 with 2,3,5,7 with 1,6,7,9: 2 x 4 x 4 x 1 = $32

Win Odds and Payouts

The following chart displays payouts based on $2 win wagers and include the $2 investment and profit.

WIN ODDS AND PAYOUTS

Odds	Payout	Odds	Payout
1-9	$2.20	2-1	$6.00
1-5	$2.40	5-2	$7.00
2-5	$2.80	3-1	$8.00
1-2	$3.00	7-2	$9.00
3-5	$3.20	4-1	$10.00
4-5	$3.60	9-2	$11.00
1-1	$4.00	5-1	$12.00
6-5	$4.40	6-1	$14.00
7-5	$4.80	7-1	$16.00
3-2	$5.00	8-1	$18.00
8-5	$5.20	9-1	$20.00
9-5	$5.60	10-1	$22.00

Handicapping

The art of predicting the winner of a horse race is called handicapping. The process of handicapping involves evaluating the demonstrated abilities of a horse in light of the conditions under which it will be racing on a given day. To gauge these abilities, handicappers use past performances, detailed published records of preceding races. These past performances indicate the horse's speed, its ability to win, and whether the performances tend to

PAYOFF: Based on a $2 wager. Includes profit and return of wager.

Odds	Payoff	Odds	Payoff	Odds	Payoff
1-9	2.20	3-1	8.00	15-1	32.00
1-5	2.40	7-2	9.00	16-1	34.00
2-5	2.80	4-1	10.00	17-1	36.00
1-2	3.00	9-2	11.00	18-1	38.00
3-5	3.20	5-1	12.00	19-1	40.00
4-5	3.60	6-1	14.00	20-1	42.00
1-1	4.00	7-1	16.00	25-1	52.00
6-5	4.40	8-1	18.00	30-1	62.00
7-5	4.80	9-1	20.00	40-1	82.00
3-2	5.00	10-1	22.00	50-1	102.00
8-5	5.20	11-1	24.00	60-1	122.00
9-5	5.60	12-1	26.00	70-1	142.00
2-1	6.00	13-1	28.00	80-1	162.00
5-2	7.00	14-1	30.00	90-1	182.00
				99-1	200.00

Bodog Sportsbook features a much more extensive payout table.

be getting better or worse. The conditions under which the horse will be racing include the quality of the competition in the race, the distance of the race, the type of racing surface (dirt or turf), and the current state of that surface (fast, good, firm, sloppy, etc).

Handicapping Variables

FITNESS – Before a horse can be considered, it should be determined that he's physically fit enough to be at or near his best. Examine the dates of prior last races. The more recent races he has, the more certain of his fitness. If he's been away from the races for two months or more, examine morning training workouts. The longer the layoff, the more difficult the comeback.

CLASS – Class is the quality of competition a horse can compete favorably against. Look at the prior conditions under which the horse has raced. Regardless of any other variable, a horse cannot be expected to win without having shown a past ability to do so against similar competition. If he has not shown the past ability, he can be considered a throw-out, unless he's rapidly improving and won his last race with enough authority to move up in class against tougher competition.

DISTANCE – Through breeding, conformation, running style, or training techniques, horses generally do better at certain distances. Few are versatile to handle short and long races effectively. Examine all races listed to determine if he's done well at the designated distance. If he's a proven competitor at today's distance, continue to consider him, and eliminate him if he's had numerous opportunities without success. Never expect a horse to do something he's never done before.

POST POSITION – As a general rule, far outside posts in bulky fields can prove more challenging. The two inside posts in big fields can also be detrimental. Early speed is favorable for both inside and outside posts because without it, outside horses lose ground and inside ones get trapped. A horse's running style and the post position are directly correlated. In longer, two-turn-races, inside posts are almost always preferred. The shorter the two-turn-race, the more it favors inside.

RUNNING STYLE – Horses generally settle into a certain style of running, broken down into three categories: pace-setter or front runner, horses who run in the lead or are never further back than two lengths; stalkers, horses who are never further back than four lengths; and closers or rally types, horses who are never closer than five lengths from the pace.

Horses have been known to change styles, but the vast majority have consistent styles. True front runners always try for the lead when possible. Front runners are most effective when unchallenged early. The easier they are able to get a clear lead, the better the chances. A stalker rarely makes the lead, and seldom possesses a big, late kick. They have the speed to stay close and pass tiring front runners, and can hold off the big closers that lag well behind. Stalkers can make the lead if no front runners are in the race. Rally or closers are best when an abundance of early speed exists and are often victimized when a front runner is loose on the lead. Statistics show that horses closer to the lead win the majority of races.

TRAINER – Give careful consideration to the trainer, who is like the coach. Some trainers are superior to others and there can be a large discrepancy between the best and the worst. Trainers have a big job and must have a wealth of knowledge about a large number of facets of training a horse to race. The trainer is responsible for all elements of the thoroughbred's career

at the racetrack, including, but not limited to, housing, feeding, training, medicating, and plotting the course of when and where to race their thoroughbred. What we see at the racetrack on race day is the result of countless hours of preparation, babysitting, and practice, between the trainer and his pupil.

JOCKEY – The role of the jockey is often understated, yet some jockeys always seem to sit atop the standings year in and year out. Yes, they win because they get the good horses, but it takes a great deal of skill to ride a horse in a race. Jockeys must possess good riding techniques, have strength, intelligence, good judgment and timing and have an ability to communicate with the horse. Some jockeys are far more proficient than others, and by perusing the statistics or by simply watching them day in and day out, you can learn which are the most reliable. Therefore, when making a final decision as to which horse you're going with for any particular race, be sure the horse you select has a good rider.

⚫ *Average height of a jockey: 5 feet, 2 inches.*
Average weight of a jockey: 105 pounds.

PRESENT FORM – When making a final selection it's important to determine that the horse is in good present form. Examining the finishes of his most recent races tells you if he's racing well and competitively. Statistics prove that horses that have recently won or have been reasonably close, win the majority of races. Most horses have form cycles in that they run well for a period of time, then tail off. Initially select horses that appear to be in form or rounding to form, and be wary of ones that have raced well, but show signs of tailing off. Sometimes horses that have not been close to winning of late are dropped in class and can still be considered viable choices, but the handicapper should expect that the horse in question at least showed some interest against better competition. Be careful not to give too much consideration to horses that are dropping down after showing no life at all as they may have lost their will to compete.

CONSISTENCY – Before considering a horse a top contender, examine his record for the year and his lifetime record. A handicapper should look for horses that are more likely to run well than not. If they have finished in the money 50 percent of the time, they can be deemed consistent. Many horses with poor consistency records cannot be heavily relied upon to run well after a good effort the time before. So, despite a good recent race, they have shown a past tendency not to repeat strong performances. A horse coming off a good race returning in a similar situation is hard to disregard. But if he's shown a lack of past consistency, his lack of reliability would make it difficult to make a serious wager on him.

WEIGHT – Some handicappers use the weight carried by a horse as a critical factor. However, determining how a few pounds, more or less, will affect a horse's performance isn't easy to assess. Race horses can weigh

well over 1,000 pounds. So humans, who generally weigh about 80% less, would find it hard to understand how 10 pounds affects a horse in comparison to a much less sturdy and strong human. Proportionately speaking, one could assume that ten pounds to a human, which is significant, may feel like only two pounds to a horse. Obviously, two pounds is hardly enough to slow him down much.

If you decide to use weight as a handicapping variable, it would seem wise to consider it more important as the length of the race increases. You may also want to use weight if comparing horses in the same race if there is a significant switch in weights, like one

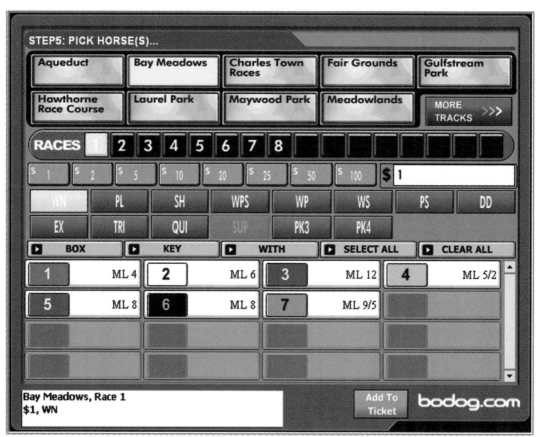

A Racebook Tote Window. You've selected your track, your race, your wager type and amount, all that's left is your horse selection.

A Race Book Ticket. Once you've selected the track and race, you're ready to bet. You will have to enter the amount you wish to wager and your wager type, then your horse number. Your next step is to "add to ticket."

horse taking off five pounds coming out of a race against a rival who may be adding five pounds.

SPEED FIGURES – Various speed figures (Beyers, etc.) have been compiled in recent years. These figures basically assign a number to each race run by a horse. Beyer numbers, for instance, are based almost exclusively by running times in conjunction with track conditions. If used, these numbers should be used more as a guide.

How to Read a Racing Form

Many serious handicappers buy the Daily Racing Form before making their picks, but for the novice bettor learning how to read the Daily Racing Form can be a daunting task. In it you'll find complete listings of past performances for all the horses entered that day, and although jam-packed with all kinds of information, the Racing Form is essentially divided into columns. The following steps may help you to better interpret what you see:

- Find the horse's name in the upper left-hand corner of the form, with the owner and trainer listed below it.
- Look for the horse's weight, color, date of birth, and breeding across from the name, reading left to right.
- Notice the sex on the upper line, listed before breeding.

- Analyze the horse's performance over the last two years using the figures in the upper right-hand corner.
- Note that the dates of previous races and their outcomes are listed in the first column on the left.
- Note the location of the race, distance and times of the race, which are shown, respectively, in the next three columns reading left to right.
- Note the track conditions in the next column.
- Read the odds for winning each race listed in the next column.
- Consider the horse's weight during each race in the next column.
- Read the next four columns. They tell you where the horse was at the one-quarter mark, the half-mile, the stretch and the finish.
- Read the next column, which indicates who the jockeys were and what their post positions were.
- Learn the classes of the races the horse has run in the next column.
- Find out the speed at which the horse ran in the various races by checking the next column.
- Review the following column, which is called "the company line." It tells you which horse won, which placed and which showed in your horse's previous races.
- Find out how many horses were in each race in the final column.

TIPS:

- Tracks listed are always abbreviated.
- A (c) means colt, which is a male horse until he turns five and becomes an (h), which means horse. A (g) indicates a gelding, which is a castrated male horse. An (f) indicates a filly, which is a female horse until she turns five and becomes an (m), which means mare.
- The little letter next to the number in the finish column indicates how the horse finished. A neck is abbreviated (nk), a head is abbreviated (h) and a nose is abbreviated (no).
- A "T" with a circle around it indicates that a race was a turf race. This means the horse ran a race on a grass track.

(Source: eHow.com)

For a complete tutorial on how to read the Daily Racing Form, go to:
www.drf.com/flash/drf_pp_tutorial.html

Glossary of Terms

Horse racing has its own lingo. For the beginner it can be a lot like trying to learn a new language. Here is a list of terms to help put you in the know:

ALLOWANCE: A race other than a claiming event for which the racing secretary drafts certain conditions.

APPRENTICE: A jockey who has ridden for less than a year and who receives weight allowances.

BAY: A color ranging from tan to dark chestnut with black mane, tail and points.

BEYER SPEED RATING: A measure of performance popularized by Andy Beyer of The Washington Post.

BOUNCE: An exceptionally poor performance following an exceptionally good one.

BROODMARE: Female horse used for breeding.

BROODMARE SIRE: A sire whose female offspring becomes producers of exceptional performers.

BULLET: Fastest workout of the day at a particular distance.

CALL TO THE POST – A special call played on a Bugle used to signal the horses to the starting gates.

CHESTNUT: A color ranging from light gold to deep red.

CLAIMING RACE: A race in which the horses are for sale at a price specified before the race. Claims are made before the race and the new owner assumes possession immediately following the race.

COLT: An ungelded horse 4 years old or younger.

DAM: The mother of a horse.

DISTAFF: A race for female horses.

DRIVING: Strong urging by the jockey.

EARLY FOOT: Good speed at the start of the race.

ENTRY: Two or more horses representing the same owner or trained by the same person and running together as a single betting interest.

INQUIRY: Official investigation of rule infractions.

FILLY: A female horse less than five years old.

FURLONG: An eight of a mile.

GELDING: A neutered male horse.

HANDICAPPING: This is the study of factors in the past performances which determine the relative qualities and abilities of horses in a race.

HANDLE: Money wagered.

JUVENILE: Two-year-old horse. It is also the age at which horses can begin racing.

MAIDEN: A horse that hasn't won a flat race in any country.

MARE: A female horse five years old or older.

MORNING LINE: The starting odds set by the track handicapper.

ODDS-ON: A horse whose odds are less than even money. A horse whose odds are 4-5 is said to be odds-on.

OFF TRACK: A track that is not fast.

OVERLAY: A horse whose odds are greater than its potential to win.

PADDOCK: Structure or area where horses are saddled and kept before going to the track.

PARI-MUTUEL: System of wagering where all the money is returned to the wagerers after deduction of track and state percentages.

PHOTO FINISH: A result so close it is necessary to use a finish-line camera to determine order of finish.

POST POSITION: A horse's position in the stating gate, numbered from the inner rail outward.

PURSE: The amount of prize money distributed to the owners of the first five or six finishers in a race (varies by state and country).

ROAN: Horse with white hairs mingled throughout its coat.

SILKS: Jacket and cap worn by jockeys.

SIRE: Father of a foal.

STALLION: Uncastrated male horse.

STUD: Stallion.

TOTE: Customers bet against each other. All the bets are pooled with deductions for costs and racing contribution. Winning dividend is calculated by dividing the remainder of the pool by the number of winning bets. Odds can change up until the start of the race.

TURF COURSE: Grass covered race course.

UNDERLAY: Horse whose odds are more promising than his potential to win.

VALET: A person who helps jockeys keep their wardrobe and equipment in order.

WEIGHT: The assigned weight for the horse, including the jockey, equipment and lead weights if needed.

YEARLING: A horse that is one year old. The universal birthdate of horses is January 1.

ONLINE BINGO

It's more popular than the movies
in the USA— all those people must
be doing something right!

ONLINE BINGO

It is often said that bingo is the best kept secret in gambling. Bet you didn't know that more people in the United States play bingo than visit movie theaters each year! Bingo? The game my grandma plays? Why on earth is it so popular?

There are three reasons: First, it's simple to play and understand. Everyone knows how to play bingo! Second, it offers all the thrills and adrenaline rush that all forms of gambling offer. And the final key reason is that it's a sociable game: People meet, chat, and support each other while they're playing, building social and emotional bonds that accentuate the experience that is bingo.

These key tenets to the popularity of bingo in the offline setting have been effectively and successfully replicated in the online environment. This successful transition from land to online has brought millions of people into the wonderful world that is online bingo. But who are these people?

Which Bingo (http://www.whichbingo.com), a major online bingo portal and a very reliable source of online bingo-specific player research, runs a continuous online survey, and its findings consist of tens of thousands of responses. Although they have data in depth, the pertinent points of their most current survey about who is playing reveal the following fascinating facts:

- 85% of online pay-to-play bingo players are female.
- 63% (almost two thirds) of online pay-to-play bingo players are aged between 35 and 54.
- 75% of online pay-to-play bingo players also play land-based bingo.
- 20% of pay-to-play respondents classify themselves a "homemakers."
- 73.2% (almost three quarters) of players play online bingo on a daily basis.

Which Bingo is a good starting point for new online bingo players.

These research findings are broadly consistent with other research findings, as well as information obtained from other online bingo sites.

So as you can see, online bingo in general terms is played by middle-aged women, with a large proportion of those classifying themselves as homemakers. A significant proportion of the people who are playing are true bingo lovers; they play in bingo halls, and they play online on a very regular basis indeed. Perhaps they even play in their sleep.

Although one could say that it is no surprise that this is what online bingo players "look like," the interesting point is that the online bingo community is completely opposite to that of almost all other forms of online gambling, which are populated by younger males with disposable income.

A Brief Overview of the Game of Bingo

Bingo is gambling's most wholesome—and most globally popular—cousin. In fact, it's one of the most popular games in the world. Land-based bingo generates more between $70 billion and $90 billion in revenue worldwide per annum. An estimated 1.6 billion people attended bingo halls across the United States in 2003. To put this in perspective, this is almost more than the amount of people who attended movie theaters and bowling alleys, combined.

Looking back, before we look forward, it is generally agreed that modern American bingo dates back to the depression years.

In 1929, A New York toy salesman named Edwin Lowe, observed a game called "Beano," which he took back home and developed into what was in its early days known as both "Housie" and "Beano" before the now recognised name of "bingo" replaced the old terminology. Previously—and to an extent still today—when one thought of bingo, it was the American Legion, the VFW Posts, church halls, and basements that sprang to mind, and a game that was a means to raise funds for the church, fire fighters, stated charities and other small groups.

In the second half of the 20th century, the casino "big boys" began bringing bingo into their product offering with glitzy halls running seven days a week and huge jackpots, car giveaways, and much more.

Now this simple but fun and acceptable type of gambling has found its way onto the Internet

Bingo made its first appearance on the Internet around 1996, although the site that claims to be the "oldest site on the Net" promotes a start date of April 1998. The sites started small, and the technology was in its infancy. By April 2000, there were only 10 pay-to-play multi-player bingo sites, but by the end of the first quarter of 2005 there were around 150 sites. Plus, there are many more access points, including:

- ⊛ AFFILIATE SITES – promotional sites that funnel players into virtual bingo halls. The operators of the affiliate sites share a portion of the money brought in by players they refer.
- ⊛ FRONT ENDS – Online bingo operators often set up numbers "front ends," which basically amount to unique URLs (Web addresses) that funnel players into a central network in the same way that affiliate sites do.
- ⊛ WHITE-LABEL SITES – The creators of bingo software license the technology to individual operators, who create unique Web sites. The front ends are skinned to create a unique gaming environment, but the back-end system is identical to those of other bingo sites using the same "white-label" software.

Whichever way the site numbers are calculated, there are still fewer bingo sites than other online gambling sites such as casinos and sports books.

So, while grandma still finds her way to the church hall to get her game on, and auntie can spend her hard-earned dollars at bingo in Vegas, mom is sitting at home staring at a PC to find her game. Before long, grandma could even be logging on for her games. If she does, as traffic trends seem to indicate she will, online bingo could be the next big thing. By some estimates, as much as 70% of players in bingo halls already play online games.

The Basics of Bingo

One of the wonderful things about bingo is its simplicity. This is also why it is such a social game; it's a great opportunity to get together with friends and play a game that doesn't require the concentration necessary to play poker or blackjack. Yet, despite its simplicity, the anticipation and build-up toward bingo in every game makes it very exciting activity.

B	I	N	G	O
3	19	32	52	63
6	22	37	57	64
7	25	FREE	58	69
12	27	42	59	70
14	28	45	60	72

An example of a typical bingo card.

The rules for traditional bingo are as such: Each player is given a card (or multiple cards) with a grid of 25 boxes (five rows and five columns). The columns are respectively represented by the letters B - I - N – G - O, and each column/letter has a range of corresponding numbers. (B: 1-15, I: 16-30, N: 31-45, G: 46-60, and O: 61-75. The number sequences for each card are unique, so no two players have matching cards. A "caller" at the front of the room selects numbers at random, based on the same number system used by the cards (B1, B2 . . . I16, I17 . . . N31, N32 . . . G 46, G47 . . . O61, O62 . . .). As the numbers are called, the players mark off the numbers on their cards when they hear them called. (The center square in the N column of every card is a free space and is, thus, always marked from the beginning.) The game ends when a player gets "BINGO," which is accomplished when a certain pattern is formed on his or her card.

B	I	N	G	O
	19		52	
6		37	57	64
7	25		58	
	27			70
14	28		60	

A winning card (by virtue of a diagonal line).

In traditional bingo, a winning pattern is five boxes in a row—vertical, horizontal or diagonal. However, there

Plus

The Letter 'X'.

Outside Picture Frame.

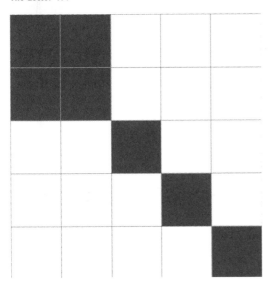

Kite.

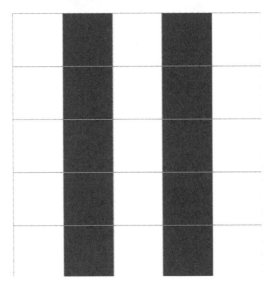

Railroad Tracks.

are countless variations of games with unique winning patterns. On this page are some of the more popular ones.

The Online Game

So how do you play this wonderful game on the Internet?

First, you must recognize that there are a variety of types of software for running Internet bingo games. This means that there may be small differences between how one game plays and how the next one plays. However, in general, they all accomplish the same thing.

Some online bingo sites offer games in a download format, meaning that the user must download and install special software before he or she can play. Once the software is downloaded, the user can then play the game whenever he or she wants without having to visit the bingo Web site. (The user still has to be connected to the Internet though.)

Other games are available in either Flash or Java, formats that don't require the user to download extra software. These games are played in the user's Web browser and are accessible through the game operator's Web site.

Like most forms of online gambling, bingo is available in free-play as well as pay-to-play formats. Even for those who wish to play for real money, it's never a bad idea to try free games first, just to get the hang of it.

On free-play sites, participants play for points, but

may also have the opportunity to compete with other players for a chance to win a variety of prizes, including small denomination cash prizes. But beware: these sites are supported by advertising revenue and sponsorship, so you will see lots of advertisements and probably receive promotional mails from pay-to-play sites.

Pay-to-play sites, on the other hand, offer the opportunity to win big cash prizes, which have been known to be as high as $30,000 for a single game.

Before you play at a pay-to-play site, you must register. This consists of supplying your name, address and email details. Sites also ask you to select an "alias" or "username" and to choose a password. After registering, you need to fund your account, and once you have done that, you can commence playing.

Most bingo sites offer a variety of games, often referred to as "streams." The streams are usually differentiated

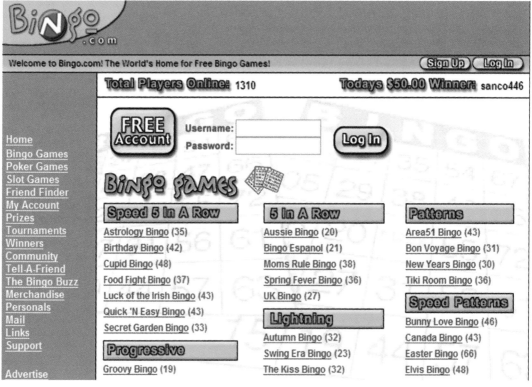

It's a good idea for new online bingo players to try a free-play site first. Bingo.com is one of many such sites.

DAUBER   SOUNDS   CHAT   HELP   NEXT ▶   EXIT

Buy Selected Cards

Quick Pick

Get New Cards

Progressive Jackpot
$10,618.29

Not in Play

Current Prize
$30.00

Time Until Game
0:39

Players
54

Player Name
elmark

Bank
$5.00

CARD# 148314 — Selected (1¢)

3	19	45	50	61
15	28	35	54	71
6	27	FREE	59	68
7	22	31	48	63
13	23	41	53	70

CARD# 148317 — Select (1¢)

9	22	42	51	72
4	21	37	56	62
8	24	FREE	47	61
11	18	32	48	70
10	16	44	46	74

CARD# 148320 — Selected (1¢)

12	21	43	51	64
15	29	44	60	74
8	28	FREE	56	75
4	27	33	54	67
1	30	40	47	65

CARD# 148323 — Select (1¢)

2	30	36	55	66
11	16	32	57	64
8	24	FREE	46	67
14	26	34	53	61
10	23	33	49	73

CARD# 148326 — Select (1¢)

11	27	36	50	66
5	21	32	55	69
8	16	FREE	53	68
13	23	34	58	75
7	22	45	49	74

CARD# 148315 — Select (1¢)

8	18	44	55	62
5	24	33	59	68
4	29	FREE	52	61
12	22	36	57	74
13	20	35	53	69

CARD# 148318 — Selected (1¢)

15	21	33	46	71
11	17	41	53	66
6	30	FREE	51	68
8	23	38	58	62
3	28	34	47	67

CARD# 148321 — Select (1¢)

14	22	34	60	67
6	30	41	56	69
3	26	FREE	51	66
2	27	33	53	61
10	23	32	59	73

CARD# 148324 — Select (1¢)

4	18	33	46	75
9	23	31	47	72
15	25	FREE	59	66
2	30	38	57	73
3	24	41	51	71

CARD# 148327 — Select (1¢)

10	27	36	50	67
1	17	32	46	66
8	25	FREE	60	74
9	24	34	47	65
2	23	39	54	75

CARD# 148316 — Select (1¢)

1	25	43	52	67
2	18	38	54	75
14	24	FREE	58	62
4	21	37	46	71
10	30	32	51	72

CARD# 148319 — Select (1¢)

14	29	43	59	73
10	19	33	56	64
8	21	FREE	46	68
2	27	36	57	75
3	18	41	49	70

CARD# 148322 — Select (1¢)

7	27	35	55	72
13	29	43	49	74
8	22	FREE	46	63
12	16	32	58	67
10	19	34	47	73

CARD# 148325 — Select (1¢)

13	25	42	57	69
9	18	37	55	66
3	26	FREE	53	75
12	22	33	51	74
4	21	35	48	71

CARD# 148328 — Select (1¢)

3	20	40	53	73
10	28	42	57	72
14	30	FREE	47	70
13	23	39	56	75
11	18	34	59	61

Before you can play, you must first purchase virtual bingo cards. FunBingo.com (pictured) allows you to view the cards before purchasing them.

either by card price (1c, 5c, 10c, 25c, 50, $1) or by type of game (coverall, shape, or speed bingo). The games are played randomly every few minutes, 24 hours a day, seven days a week. Having selected your game stream, the bingo game interface automatically loads with virtual bingo tickets that can be used to play in the next game. To join, all you need to do is click the tickets you wish to play and then click on the purchase button.

> Online bingo enables you to play many games at once without going crazy trying to cover them all simultaneously. Just select the "automatic daub" feature and let the software do the work for you.

When the game begins, the software's "caller" announces the balls as they come out. Each number that's called appears on the call board as they are announced. Most software will "daub" (mark off) the called numbers that match the numbers on your bingo ticket automatically. As with "real" bingo the game finishes when a player completes either the shape or coverall and the software automatically "calls" bingo for the player.

Each site has its own "flavor," with unique graphics, card presentation and themes. Within the game card frame there are usually various options available;

Features to look for in a good site include:

- Choice of caller voice
- Choice of color and/or dauber shape
- Best card first
- Autodaub
- Auto forward purchasing

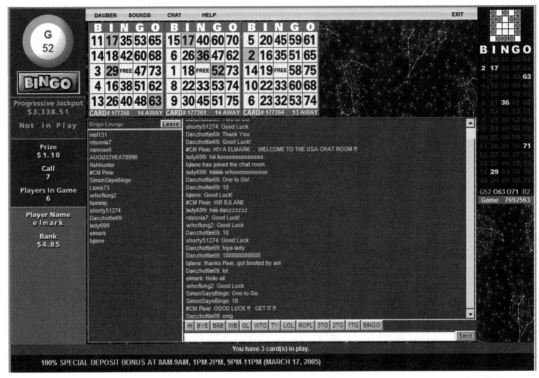

FunBingo.com's bingo software makes it easy to keep track of the action during game play. Your cards, your bank roll, the selection of balls, the sequence of balls picked and a chat window can all be viewed simultaneously.

- Sound on/off
- Number of spaces to go until bingo
- Variable chat fonts and emoticons

One simply needs to check them all out to get a feel for what works best, and then he or she is off and playing. Some cards will even change colors when they down to three to go, two to go and one to go... and the much desired red for BINGO!

As mentioned, just like real bingo, online bingo is a social activity. Players often say that they play at one Internet bingo site rather than another because their friends play there—and these are often people they've never met in the flesh.

The social side of online bingo takes place in the chat window. Chat is an integral part of any online bingo game. It enables players to communicate with the "chat managers" (CMs), friends, and other players, ultimately bringing the bingo hall atmosphere into the comfort of the players' homes. Players usually have an option regarding whether they are in the chat room. However, players in a chat room are under no obligation to participate in chat. To take part in a conversation, simply type your message in the small box at the bottom of the chat window and click "send." The chat managers are usually available 24/7 to help you get involved. You'll recognize them by the different color type and/or the "CM" in front of their names.

Enhancing Your Online Bingo Experience

With 150-plus online bingo sites out there to choose from, you're probably wondering where you should play. A comprehensive list of all pay-to-play bingo sites can be found in the directory section of WhichBingo (http://www.whichbingo.com). But the most important thing to remember is that bingo is a community game, and boy, can that community chat! So take advantage of it. If a site is a scam, or is a particularly slow at paying out winnings, you can be pretty sure that you'll hear or read about. Conversely, the good payers, big jackpots, best bonuses and most welcoming communities will also be found on the game's grapevine. So explore the many forums, read the player reviews and generally get a feel for what is out there. Check out the editorial sections of sites like WhichBingo to view analysis of the key sites and announcements of all the new sites and the best offers. WhichBingo even has a section that allows players to submit their own reviews of sites.

You'll also soon find that the quality of any bingo site is determined greatly by its chat room. Take a look at CM of the Year (www.cmoftheyear.com), a site dedicated to chat room managers (hence the title). If a CM is highlighted on this site, you can bet the chat room, and thus the game, is a good one. There's also a very popular forum there that's worth checking out.

Finally, if you want to get the scoop on which sites might best be avoided, check out the 'Bingo Grumbles' section of the portal OnlineBingo.net. The forum there is recognized as the place to go to warn others of potential hazards. There's also a "praise the site" section, which is a good counter-balance.

So, once you've checked out the forums and listened

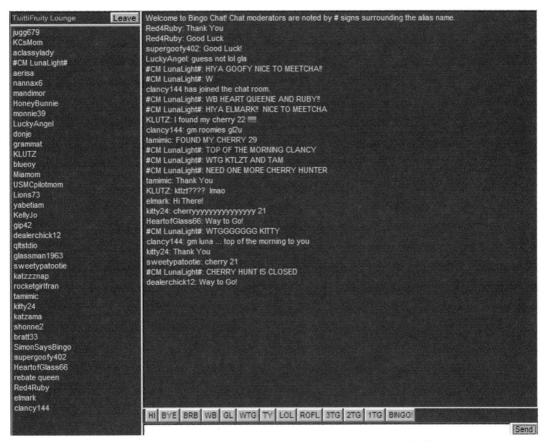

It's not online bingo unless there's chatting... and plenty of it. Pictured here is a chat window at FunBingo.com.

to the gossip, what's the next step in making sure you get the most out of your bingo buck? Here are four handy tips:

- ⊛ PLAY FOR FREE FIRST. Most sites offer the opportunity to play for free before you make a deposit. Those that offer this have a separate room or stream that is free to play and has no prize money. It's there to give the player a chance to get a feel for the software. Do you like it? Does it feel comfortable playing? Is it easy to use? Does your PC like it? Take up the offer and play for free as long as you wish.

- ⊛ TAKE THE MONEY. In addition to the free play, most sites now also offer a limited amount of free money or cards to play with before you deposit. Again, this gives you a feel for the game but even more so because you are now playing in the game proper. Thus you can play the game without risking your own money. But note you will not be able to withdraw any money if you are lucky enough to win a game.

- ⊛ LOOK AT THE DEPOSIT OFFER. All sites offer a bonus on your first deposit as well as subsequent ones, and these bonuses are becoming more and more generous. Shop around and you should be able to find some good ones. But take note, restrictions exist on withdrawals. Read the terms of the bonus BEFORE you play. You may well also be lucky enough to receive a free gift (t-shirt etc.) depending on the value of your deposit. Do remember that sites do not give FREE money. The bonuses are there to encourage you to play, and stay. They are not a free lunch!

- ⊛ HOW BIG IS THE JACKPOT? As online bingo has grown so have the jackpots on offer. We're all in it to win the money, so why not just play at the sites with the biggest jackpots?

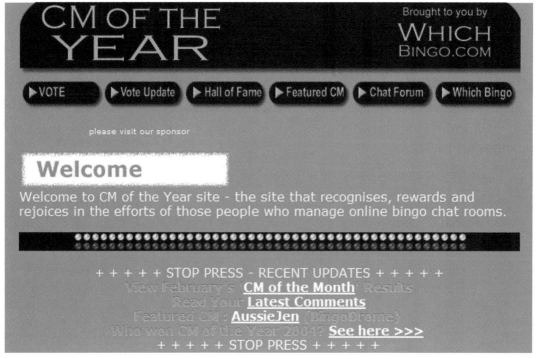

Do you know where the good CM's are hiding? "CM of the Year" will help you find them.

You should now be in a position to make a well informed choice as to where to play, but how do you increase your chances of winning? Well, the bad news is that however you cut it, and wherever you play, bingo is a game of luck. If the bingo gods are looking favorably down on you, then that last ball you require for the big jackpot will be called. If they are not... well, there's always the next game.

That said, a number of factors could enhance your experience—and perhaps even your chances for that big win. First, the more participants, the bigger the pots. So look at the number of people playing before you join a game. Conversely, if there are too many people playing, your chances of winning are reduced. Second, 90% of progressive jackpots that are won total $5,000 or less. So if you see a site with a progressive jackpot over the magical $5,000 mark, then it's more likely to drop. So, buy more cards for the big jackpot games than for the smaller ones. The more cards you buy, the more chance you have of winning. Remember each card statistically has the same chance of winning. More cards = more chance. But don't overdo it. Always check how much your purse can comfortably provide for entertainment. If you play with money that you know you have allocated for entertainment, then it won't hurt has much if you lose. Next, play the right games; according to one site's research, fast games that have less than 10 dots on the pattern, are more likely to be progressive jackpot winners than others.

Finally, the key thing to remember is that bingo is a social game. Regardless of whether you're winning, the important thing is to have fun. Many bingo players choose where they are going to play online based on where their friends from all over the Internet are playing, and the environment of the chat rooms. If they like the chat rooms and the chat master, then they will keep coming back to play. You might not become a millionaire, but you'll have lots of fun and meet loads of great people from around the world!

Best of bingo luck!

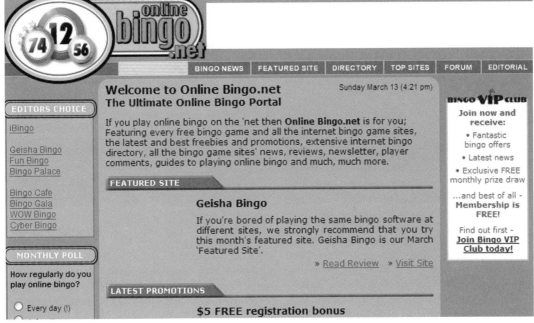

Word of mouth is a powerful thing on the Internet. Sites like OnlineBingo.net give players a voice and enable them to warn other players of sites they should avoid.

LOTTERIES

Lottery found its way to the internet before any other form of gambling in September 1995 from the tiny principality of Liechtenstein in the heart of Europe. Liechtenstein charity foundation ILLF (the International Lottery in Liechtenstein Foundation, www.illf.com) launched the world's first credible Internet gaming site as www.interlotto.li. It was renamed "PLUS Lotto" (www.pluslotto.com) in 1997, and a relationship was established with the International Federation of Red Cross and Red Crescent Societies as the principal beneficiaries.

Interlotto had a relatively slow start, with the many of players scared to use credit cards on the Internet in the earlier years and access speeds relatively slow. From an initial format of a single weekly CHF 5 per entry (Swiss Franc) lotto style 6/40 game, the site grew to encompass scratch cards and other innovative instant games, including pachinko, higher frequency games, keno and instant bingo.

PLUS Lotto picked up where Interlotto left off in 1997.

In 2000, ILLF introduced the concept of white-labelling and added a number of themed and speciality lotteries in partnership with third-party marketing partners. One of the most interesting partners was www.wildlifewins.com, a site dedicated to wildlife conservation. Unfortunately, due to insufficient marketing funds, the site failed and was withdrawn in 2002. Other brands launched under the ILLF umbrella include www.lottoluck.com, www.globelot.com and www.planetlotto.com.

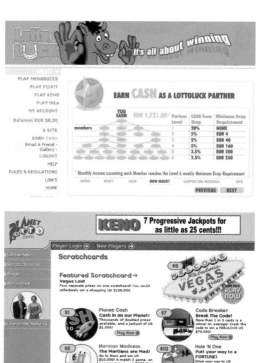

Some that Came and Went

In 1997 ILLF saw its first direct competition from www.USLottery.com – an instant 6/49 game operated by the Coeur D'Alene Indian tribe in Idaho. This operated for about a year before being closed due to legal challenges from US regulators. Operator eLottery went

Lotto Luck, Planet Lotto, and Globelot are three of several lottery sites launched under the ILLF umbrella.

on to offer the software to the Jamaica lottery where it operated for a number of years.

www.InterKeno.com started in 1996 with a keno-style lotto game operating out of Gibraltar, went through an identity crisis as Casares.com, but eventually folded through lack of volume.

The Postcode Lottery operator Novamedia from the Netherlands launched at considerable expense their Internet site www.goodlot.com but never had a great deal of success with it.

STATE/NATIONAL LOTTERIES – Terrestrial lotteries have been slow to come online, largely because of slow regulatory changes and an ethic of civil service in management. It is now possible, however, to play many of the European state lotteries online in one way or another. Some have a different game set for the Internet, and they all restrict access to players from other countries. There are currently no US lotteries operating on the internet due to legal restrictions.

Norway's Veikkaus was one of the first European state lotteries to offer lottery tickets. Camelot in the UK began selling weekly lotto tickets in 2003 (their license was renewed with a requirement that they sell online) and now also sells scratch cards online. Both the Austrian and French lotteries use software from Access gaming to offer scratch card and instant games.

Games from the state lotteries include weekly lotto, scratch cards and smaller numbers games. In general,

due to their restrictive licences, state lotteries tend to offer lower payouts than can be found at the ILLF games or through soft gaming sites such as Jackpotjoy.

SOFT GAMING – Soft gaming has a substantial crossover with the Internet lottery space; both offer very similar games, the former through lottery licenses and the latter through fixed-odds bookmaker licenses. The precise definition of soft gaming isn't essential for casual bettors to know, but the basic idea is that the laws in certain jurisdictions (the UK being the prime example) allow fixed-odds betting services to offer certain electronic fixed-odds games, such as slots, keno and other "fixed-odds" games, while casino games such as blackjack, craps and roulette can online be offered at casinos. Most UK bookmakers offer soft gaming. Jackpotjoy.com specializes in this area.

MOBILE LOTTERIES – Pluslotto launched a number of WAP sites with limited success and still operates a WAP version of its games at mobile.pluslotto.com. SMS ticket entry has been available for some time at many national lotteries; typically, players register their number selections and payment details in advance on a Web site and then purchase these tickets by sending an SMS text message. Payment is still effected off the Internet account. Additionally, a new SMS-based lottery, SMSLottome, was launched in the UK in 2005. (Later we look at mobile gambling—including the WAP and SMS protocols—in further detail.)

What's Available Now

WEEKLY LOTTO – Most people think of weekly lotto when they think of lotteries. The weekly lotto has been around for many years in many countries and states around the world. In fact, lottery is probably one of the oldest forms of gambling. In the Book of Numbers, God directs Moses to divide land among the Israelites by drawing lots. Roman emperors gave away land and slaves via lotteries during feasts. China's Hun Dynasty created keno to finance the construction of the Great Wall.

Weekly lotto relies on a large player base, taking entry fees from many players and then returning prizes to a few based on the matching of numbers. Without a large player base, it is impossible to generate the liquidity to support the large prizes. A new innovation on the Internet, pioneered by ILLF and later copied by free lotteries, is to insure the jackpot prize with a suitable prize indemnity insurance company. This way it is possible to offer jackpots that exceed the ticket sales, leveraging off the fact that the game is purely random and the odds are relatively easy to calculate. Needless to say, it is critical for the insurance company that the game is fairly conducted; in some respects an insured jackpot can be taken as an endorsement of the operator's integrity and controls.

A player's odds of winning any high jackpot game are quite long by design. If it was easy to win, huge jackpots would not be possible! One thing to look for in lottery is the secondary prizes. With games such as Megabucks on the Internet offering an even-money return for a two-ball match, the proposition becomes more attractive. By far, the worst payouts are from the free or subscription lotteries (hardly surprising). High payout games such as Powerball and Euro Millions are designed to be less intimidating by separating the number selection into an initial selection and a secondary qualifier (the Powerball, or Stars in Euro Millions). To calculate the odds in these games one has to multiply the odds of the initial game by the qualifier.

To give some idea as to the odds of winning see Table 1 below.

SCRATCH CARDS – Scratch cards are a phenomenon particularly well suited to the corner store and do not translate that well to the Internet. Although many lotteries sell scratch cards online, with the UK National lottery "Monopoly" game being one of the more interesting versions, they are generally not competitive against other newer style Internet-only games. That is not to say the UK National Lottery does not sell a lot of Internet scratch cards; with a monopoly in the United

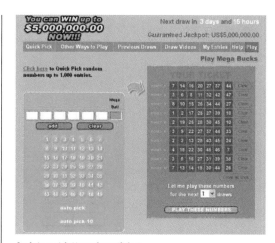

An Internet lottery draw ticket.

Kingdom and a huge offline marketing budget, their games do not have to be as competitive as an Internet-only site. But in general, given the choice, players prefer the more interactive and complex games that are possible on the Internet today.

MORE FREQUENT LOTTO – Daily and hourly games are offered by some state lotteries as well as Pluslotto. These are typically easier to win than the weekly game, with a commensurate reduction in the jackpot size. Little Big One on the Pluslotto site has long been a favourite. Available every hour on the half hour, the game has had over 73,000 draws. With a 5/15 draw format, the odds of winning the jackpot are 1 in 3003. One trick is to wait for the jackpot to exceed $2,000 and then purchase every ticket in the next game. If you are the only person doing this, your winnings will be as follows:

Cost of tickets = $3,003. Winnings = Rollover +

Table 1: ODDS OF WINNING

Type	Odds of winning jackpot	Some lotteries that offer this game
6/45	1 in 8,145,060	Swiss Lotto
6/49	1 in 13,983,816	UK National Lottery, Lottoluck Megabucks
Euro Millions	1 in 76,275,360	United Kingdom, France, Spain, Austria, Belgium, Ireland, Luxembourg, Portugal, Switzerland
Powerball	1 in 120,526,770	Some US States
Mega Millions	1 in 135,145,920	Some US States

65% of amount played = $2,000 + $1,951 = $3,951.

There is a risk, however, that you end up sharing the jackpot with another player. This can be mitigated by monitoring the speed at which the jackpot increases hour on hour. The smaller the hourly increase in jackpot size, the smaller the number of players during that period.

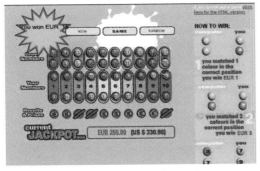

Instant games, like "Snowball" are quite popular among online lottery players.

60 SECOND FIXED-ODDS GAMES – Ladbrokes pioneered the fixed-odds, betting style known as "1-minute lotto" in 2001 with the launch of their "Balls" game. All the other UK bookmakers followed them and there are now a number of variations on this game now available, including the original "Balls" game (www.ladbrokes.com), Coral Eurobet's "60 Seconds" (www.eurobet.com) and LottoLuck's "Pick!t" (www.lottoluck.com).

All these games share a similar method of operation: Numbers are drawn every minute, and players can bet on a wide variety of aspects including colours, total score, combinations of numbers and other similar bets. In a way these games combine roulette with lotto by offering roulette-style bets in a lotto-style draw. "Pick!t" extends this further by offering a user interface that would be familiar to a roulette player.

"Pick!t" also offers a lotto game across multiple draws, called "Pick!t Lotto," in which you pick a number that you think will appear in the next five consecutive draws. The prize is the jackpot displayed in the game and is supplemented with contributions from all other games on "Pick!t" so the game pays out over 100% at times. The hugely popular game's jackpot goes

down a few times every day and averages a few thousand euros or dollars.

Take care to note the numeric range on which you're betting, as this affects the payout on all the bets. Ladbrokes "Balls" has the longest odds with 6 from 48, followed by Coral Eurobet "60 Seconds" with 6 from 37 and LottoLuck "Pick!t" with 6 from 30.

It won't make you a millionaire, but Pick!t offers lucky gamblers a quick ride to a nice little chunk of change.

HILO – This is offered in many different forms, again through bookmaker's soft games sites as well as at LottoLuck, where the game resembles a slot machine and there are additional jackpots available for all 4 "reels" (producing the same number or all 4 "reels" coming up with 7).

When playing HiLo, you're betting on a single number coming out higher or lower than the previous one. One caution: Most software automatically makes your previous winnings the current stake. It's worth cashing out and starting again at a lower stake if you have accumulated a decent stake rather than risking losing it all.

KENO – Keno is a fixed-odds lottery game offered on virtually every casino on the Internet. It's hugely popular in Australia, where it's available in social clubs with countrywide jackpots. Most online casinos don't offer keno games with pari-mutuel jackpots, rather they offer

HiLo is on of many "soft" games attracting gamblers looking for more than traditional lottery games.

it as a pure fixed-odds game. On ILLF, the game is available with a number of jackpots. The odds in keno are very long, but are mitigated by the lower number of match payouts.

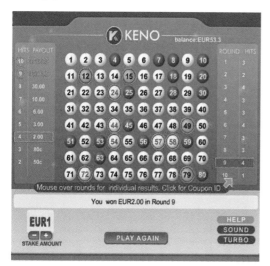

Online casinos aren't the only sites that offer keno. The game is also available at sites that offer soft games, such as LottoLuck.com

MOBILE GAMES – WAP-based scratch cards and a numbers game are available via soft games providers such as mobile.pluslotto.com. Users must have an account at the Internet site and can then play mobile games against this account. Many state and national lotteries offer ways to purchase tickets online; varying from country to country. They typically only offer a weekly lotto game.

SMSLottome is a mobile game that's a bit different. It can be played by anyone with a UK mobile phone (they have plans to expand into Europe) and does not require any pre-registration or payment. Players send an SMS with the word 'Lottome' followed by either three, four or five digits to the entry number. This enters them into one of three draws. The three-digit code is matched against the system generated numbers in the next draw (draws take place every minute) and players can win up to £250. The four-digit code can win £2,500 and the five-digit code £30,000. The four-digit game is drawn hourly, while the five-digit game is drawn daily.

Other Important Features

CHARITY – Lotteries traditionally contribute to charity or good causes. Look for information on the site as to where the good cause funds are going. All state lotteries publish their contributions. ILLF publishes its beneficiaries and donation amounts on www.illf.com.

REFERRAL REWARDS – These are commissions paid to players that refer other players and range from a relatively simple percentage or amount per ticket or player to a more complex model such as the multi-level model found on LottoLuck.

LOTTERY TICKET RESELLERS – There are many agents who offer chances to participate in various state lotteries around the world by reselling the tickets. While some of these are credible, they generally price the tickets substantially higher than the retail cost. For example, one site at the time of going to press offered one game for four weeks in the UK lottery for $69. That is an £8 cost (to draws for four weeks) retailing for £36.34! Beware sites that offer a "basket" of tickets from a number of different lotteries, often combining different currencies. Offering a strange number of tickets (such as eight in each draw) and combining many currencies are often means of disguising substantial mark-ups. There is also a question as to the legality of tickets being resold

LottLuck has a tiered rewards system.

EARN CASH AS A LOTTOLUCK PARTNER

YOU EARN EUR 1,731.00*

Partner Level	CASH from Drop	Minimum Drop Requirement
1	20%	NONE
2	5%	EUR 4
3	5%	EUR 40
4	5%	EUR 160
5	2.5%	EUR 200
6	2.5%	EUR 250

members

*Monthly income assuming each Member reaches the Level 6 weekly Minimum Drop Requirement

INTRO   HOW?   CASH   **HOW MUCH?**   SUPPORTING MATERIAL   JOIN

PREVIOUS   NEXT

SELECT
PLAY MEGABUCKS
PLAY PICKIT
PLAY KENO
PLAY HiLo
MY ACCOUNT
Balance: EUR 58.30
$ SITE
EARN CASH
Email A Friend -
Gallery -
LOGOUT
HELP
RULES & REGULATIONS
LINKS
HOME

on the Internet. All state and national lotteries prohibit sales to non-residents. Resellers get around this restriction by claiming to be a syndicate (so the ticket is shared with them) and taking a percentage of all prizes. In general, players that reside in a jurisdiction where it is possible to play the lottery are far better off purchasing an entry into a multi-state game such as Powerball or Euromillions at their local grocery store.

FREE LOTTERIES – Free lotteries hit the Internet with a vengeance around 1999. Offering the chance to win large prizes to players who clicked on an advertising banner to play, they were an effective means of marketing for a few years. But over time, players started to realize how hard it is to win at these high odds (bear in mind that, unlike state lotteries or those from ILLF, free lotteries typically only pay winnings to top prize winners). Free lotteries still enjoy a place on the Internet, but their appeal has waned. Luckysurf, one of the oldest free lotteries, added a subscription option to their game

whereby players could subscribe for automatic entry in the game rather than click banners. This effectively moved the funding of the jackpot from the advertisers back to the player and is actually a sweepstake (thus falling into a different legal area to lottery). The small price paid per entry (around $0.13) is indicative of the amount that goes to the top jackpot in all lottery games.

What to Look for in a Lottery Site

It goes without saying that players coming across an Internet lottery for the first time should ensure that the lottery is licensed and operated by a credible operator. State lottery sites tend to have the largest jackpots, but the worst odds, particularly for instant games. Other important qualities are much the same as those important for any type of gambling. Ease and access to payments, game choice and customer support come into play at lottery sites just as they do at online casinos, sports books and other sites where you can gamble online.

MAHJONG!

The fascinating game of Mahjong has roots in Asia and has become one of the most widely played games throughout the world. Played by beginners and masters alike, it is based on an easily understood proposition (similar to Rummy), but intriguingly, the game can take years to master. With its exciting combination of skill, luck and karma, the game of Mahjong always means something personal to the many regular players.

The origins of the game are shrouded in mystery. According to one theory, the game was played during the 40 days and nights on Noah's Ark, that would suggest the game dates back to 235 BC. Another supposes that the game was invented by the great philosopher Confucius around 500 BC. A more likely theory is that the game developed from earlier Chinese games such as

Ya Pei and Ma Tiae and that around 1850 AD the game of Mahjong was formalized as we know it today.

During the 1920s the game was introduced into the United States and became mainstream and very popular. Indeed, such was the demand for Mahjong sets, they became the 6th most valuable export commodity from Shanghai. Amongst others Parker Brothers and Milton

The players are seated at the start of the game.

Bradley also began production of Mahjong sets and it is said that the demand for the production actually saved Milton Bradley from bankruptcy.

It seemed that most American establishments where the game was played decided to adopt their own set of rules. That was until 1924 when the official American rule book was published in an attempt to standardize the way the game is played. There are however many rule sets in common use today; these include the most popular Hong Kong Cantonese game as well as the Shanghai, Japanese, and Taiwanese versions (to name a few).

Game Introduction

The game is played with a set of Mahjong tiles which were originally made of bone, ivory or bamboo and more recently from high quality plastics. The sound of the tiles when shuffled together resembles that of birds chirruping and chattering and hence the name Mahjong which in English literally means "Hemp Bird" or more commonly "Sparrow."

Examination of a standard Mahjong set will show 144 tiles in total, and these are divided up into "common tiles" of three suites and "honor tiles" of Dragons and Winds. Additionally there are "seasons" and "flowers." The three suites are "Characters," "Circles," and "Bamboos," and each consists of numbered tiles from 1 to 9. (There are four of them each.) Then there are three types of Dragon: Red, White and Green. There are four types of Wind: East, West, North and South. Optionally, there is one of each season tile—Spring, Summer,

The wall is broken, and the players are dealt 13 tiles with one extra for the dealer—the East wind.

Autumn, and Winter—as well as four flower tiles: Plum, Orchid, Chrysanthemum, and Bamboo. A typical Mahjong set contains 144 tiles.

The optional flowers and season tiles are Spring, Summer, Autumn, Winter, Plum, Orchid, Chrysanthemum and Bamboo. There is one tile of each, and not four as in the other tiles. These tiles can be incorporated in a game if the players agree. They act as a kind of bonus tile; they are not incorporated in the player's Mahjong hand but placed face up in front of the player and another tile is drawn from the tail of the wall.

The traditional Hong Kong Cantonese Mahjong game requires that four players sit at a square table; their seating positions are known as the winds: East, South, West and North. At the beginning of a game, each player is randomly seated and the player that has been allocated the East seat is the dealer. A Mahjong game usually consists of at least four "rounds," in which each player is East Wind at least once. If the East Wind player wins, he can retain East Wind for another round, so a game can consist of more than four rounds of Mahjong. Hereafter, a round is referred to as a game.

Tradition dictates that the tiles are shuffled face down and that each of the four players create a wall of tiles— two high and 18 long (17 if the optional Flowers and Seasons are not included). The four walls are then placed together to create a square wall.

Thirteen tiles are be dealt to each player, with one extra for the dealer, but first the ritual of "breaking the wall" is

In an Internet multiplayer game, the central game server has to make sure all players are ready to start.

Play proceeds in a counterclockwise direction. The previous player discarded the 1 of characters, and this is now offered as a Cheung or Chow.

carried out to decide where the dealing should begin. The position of the break is decided by the roll of two dice.

The general idea of the game is to assemble a winning Mahjong hand before the other players. This is done by picking up and discarding tiles according to the player's strategy and it is this decision-making process of which tiles to keep and which to discard that is the essence of the game. Once the tiles are dealt, the player decides on his or her strategy.

Although there are a few exceptions, most winning Mahjong hands consist of 3s of a kind (called a "Pong"), straights (called a "Chow"), and/or 4's of a kind (called a "Kong"). A Kong is actually counted as three tiles, and should a player achieve a "Kong," he is dealt another tile. A winning hand consists of any combination of four Pongs, Chows or Kongs and a pair of tiles called the "Eyes." That's 14 tiles (always counting a Kong as 3 tiles).

A CHICKEN HAND is an unremarkable mixture of Pongs and Chows.

Scoring

Scoring is reasonably straightforward. A winning Mahjong hand and the circumstances that lead up to its achievement dictate the number of Fans the hand is worth. The lowest Fan score is 0 for what's called a "Chicken Hand," and the highest is 15. Fans are translated into points, which go up more or less exponentially for each extra Fan that is achieved. So for one Fan, you would receive 4 points and for six Fans 65 points, right up to 15 Fans for 1,536 points. The idea behind all of this is to encourage the players to achieve the highest number of Fans by going for the most difficult of hands and to maintain a discipline in doing so.

Optional variations to the scoring can be such that players have "accounts" and pay the points from their accounts to the winner. In this case, the discarder of a tile that is used by the winning player to complete his hand (known as "Winning by Discard") can be punished by being made to pay all of the points to the winner. More commonly, he may pay the larger part of the winning points with the other losers paying the smaller part. Should the winner win by picking a tile from the wall (known as winning by "Self Pick"), the three losing players pay equally.

Strategy Outlined

Once dealt a Mahjong hand, a player works out a strategy to return the maximum value in the fastest time for that combination of tiles. The easiest hands are usually obtained faster but these tend to score low— the lowest scoring hand being a Chicken Hand, which gives 0 Fans or 2 points. The more difficult high scoring hands take longer to achieve but can be well worth the risk. A Chicken Hand player needs to win many more times than the player who occasionally obtains a high scoring hand.

Avoid collecting suits that other players are collecting by taking note of their discards. Another clue to a

The player opts to take the Chow – laid down on the table.

Players are dealt tiles (as in the Red Dragon on the right), and can choose to discard a tile by clicking it with the mouse.

player's intentions is when a player lays down two or more triplets of one suit. Avoid collecting that suit, but be careful with your discards.

Maximizing the Ways to Go Mahjong

The fourteenth tile completes a Mahjong hand, which is generally four triplets and a pair. Maximizing the ways to complete the hand means maximizing the different tiles that would qualify the hand as a winner. If only one tile qualifies the hand, such as waiting for the other half of the pair, then care must be taken to ensure that some tiles are still left in the wall. Remember the remainder could be in the other players' hands, and the tile may never come free. This could mean that the hand can never win.

A better way is to end up waiting for a Chow, such as a 4 and 5. Then the hand needs a 3 or a 6 to win, and this can be picked up from any player's discard, as the tile will qualify a hand for Mahjong. The same goes for waiting for a tile to complete one of two Pongs; either of two tiles could win the game.

Let's say a hand has three completed triplets and a 1 x 5 and a triplet of 6s. The hand is waiting on a 5 to make the pair, but also on a 7 as this would make 5,6,7 and a pair of 6s. Plus, a 4 would be excellent as well, as this would make 4,5,6 and a pair of 6s. In this case, there are three different tiles to go Mahjong, which is much better than just waiting for a pair!

It's all about winning. Here, the East wind is discarded and can be picked up by "our" player to win the game.

Mahjong on the Internet

The popularity of the Internet enables people from all over the world to play against one another from the comfort of their own futons. Mahjong works well on the Internet. All the hard work of shuffling and dealing of tiles is done for the player, and all the fun of the game is still there. Also, the scores for each winning hand are handled automatically and correctly. All that's left for the player to do is to concentrate on playing a skilful game.

There are a number of great Web sites where many players come to pit their skills against one another. Most of them require players to register their names and addresses, and in return they receive usernames and passwords to access the site. A download of the Web site's gaming software is usually required, and once the

software is installed, the player can play online against other Internet Mahjong players.

The Internet Mahjong player can choose from three main types of sites:

- FREE SITES – Play whenever you want for free (usually against a computer).
- SUBSCRIPTION SITES – Mainly consisting of real multiplayer tournaments
- MAHJONG CLUB SITES – Straight game betting propositions and tournaments.

All three types are popular, with some sites showing over 30,000 players online at any given moment.

Fundamentally, two forms of Mahjong are available online for money or prizes: the single Mahjong game and the Mahjong tournament. With a straight game of

The Result Page at the end shows how clever a player can be!

Mahjong, each player risks a fixed stake on the outcome of a game, and the winner receives payment from the others. The player is not rewarded for the elegance of his Mahjong hand, only for the fact that he has a Mahjong hand at all. The skill in is to think fast and play fast.

In a tournament, the game is played using traditional scoring and is played over the traditional minimum four rounds of Mahjong. At the end of the tournament, points are added up and the top players are rewarded with cash and/or other prizes.

The Internet presents some problems, mainly related to security, trust and collusion. On the whole, the Internet Mahjong player should only play on sites that have a recognized name and a reputable history. You can be sure that their software will not compromise your computer and that all communications with the central server are encrypted, thus denying any hacker the ability to trace your network traffic.

While these rules are general for all Internet activity, Mahjong has specific risks associated with collusion among players (when two or more secretly try and help each other to win). The rules forbid this of course, but it is difficult to detect. Some Mahjong Web sites employ game rules that make the discarder of the winning tile pay the full penalty to the winner, thereby removing the advantage. Other techniques involve artificial intelligence systems to detect collusion. Details of these are understandably sketchy. Any player caught colluding is disqualified from the tournament and typically banned from the Web site.

SKILL GAMES

Play your favorite game on the Web. Play that game against someone thousands of miles away. Play that same person for money. The concept seems simple enough, and its growing popularity is booming with some estimates putting the online gaming industry (not including gambling) at a two billion dollar a year business within the next thirty months. This type of gaming is expected to dominate the future and create an entirely new form of entertainment.

What is Skill Gaming?

The term "Online Skill-Based Games" refers specifically to online skill games that are offered in a cash tournament model, in which players pay cash entry fees to play against other players in the hopes of winning cash or merchandise prizes. Some of these games are directly head-to-head experiences (e.g. chess), and others are essentially single-player experiences where a player's score is compared against other players' scores to determine a winner or winners. This is compared to online gambling where consumers play against algorithm-based casino-type games.

Skill gaming is legal in most jurisdictions within the North America, Europe and Asia, and transactions for these sites are accepted by major banks and processors, including MasterCard, Visa, Diners, Amex and third-party payment processors like PayPal and NETeller.

While publicly traded companies in the skill gaming arena—such as CYOP Systems (SkillArcade.com) and Fun Technologies (SkillJam.com)—are processing transactions through major US financial institutions, most of these institutions do not process transactions for online gambling sites. This can make it difficult sometimes for online gamblers to use their credit cards, as some online gambling sites are experiencing up to an 80% decline rate on North American credit card.

What separates skill-based gaming from "gambling" is the element of skill involved across all games. Skill

The Industry

Online skill gaming has been defined as a sector of the video game industry, which has been called "recession proof" by some Wall Street analysts and the video game industry is now larger than the entire film industry and is growing at a rate of between 10 to 20% per year. Combined with the emergence of consol-based gaming such as X-Box and PS2 and the growing popularity of wireless games, this industry is expected to be the dominant form of entertainment on the Internet by 2006.

games are predominantly based upon a player's logic, speed, dexterity and so forth, whereas traditional casino games rely primarily upon chance. Gambling, by its very definition, is any activity involving chance, consideration and reward. By definition, skill gaming eliminates the elements of chance.

The evolution of online gaming began in the mid-90s with free games on sites such as Pogo, Yahoo, and Riddler.com. Rather than charge people to play, these portals derived their income through advertising revenue (banners, e-mail database rentals, etc.). But the online advertising industry collapsed in 2002, forcing many play-for-free operators to charge monthly memberships for games. Combined with a crackdown in North America by credit card companies on Internet gambling, this lead to the growth of skill gaming. In 2002, major console providers introduced monthly fees for the right to play games online against other online users. The natural evolution is a combination of online console gaming with the ability to play for more that bragging rights: the ability to wager in real-time against competitors.

Now the industry is not far from taking games like SOCOM™, Halo™ and Half Life™ and allowing players to compete for cash. CYOP Systems' game Urban Mercenary™, which was built on the Quake I Platform, is an example of the emergence of head-to-head video game competitions for money in real-time on the Internet.

Other games that are available in the skill format include trivia; action games such as Donkey Kong™, Asteroids™; adventure games like Doom; and strategy games such as Mahjong and Solitaire. Most games are built in Shockwave and Java with download sizes of well under 1 megabyte.

How to win money

In order to offer tournament games with a cash entry fee and a cash prize, performance is based on a player's skill level and not just elements of luck and randomness. A typical skill game tournament takes between one and three minutes; a single tournament may have as many as twenty players participating within a thirty-second period. Therefore, skill games also provide a high entertainment value because they provide many games per hour. Furthermore, in a game like blackjack, the house wins on average 98.3% of the

Pyramid Solitaire is one of many real-money skill games available on the Internet.

time, whereas in the skill gaming the house charges a fee to enter and the entire prize pool is awarded to the players. Every skill tournament player pays the entrance fee and then a second amount for the prize pool. The prize pool goes to the winners, while the entire entrance fee goes to the house.

Think of it this way: You and a friend go into a video arcade and play a video game. You each have to plug 25 cents into the machine. That is your entrance fee and goes to cover the cost of running the tournament, software, and so forth. You then each place a side bet of $1. This $2 amount is prize pool. Then you play the game, and the person with the highest score wins the $2.

Another example is playing golf in a tournament where there is a prize for the best golfer. In this tournament, four players are given a certain amount of time to finish the game. You pay your entrance fee (green fee) and play 18 holes. Sometime during the course of the allotted time, the other contestants play their 18 holes, and when all have finished, the winner is announced.

This is how skill tournaments work on the Internet for games like Solitaire or Collapse. You don't actually have to play head-to-head in real time. All you are trying to do is get the highest score for the tournament that you signed up for.

Skill gaming software is based on the individual player's skill and knowledge, while most games of chance on the Internet are based on algorithms. Several sets of criteria are introduced that make skill-bingo, for example, a competitive game played in tournaments or head to head, where skill, knowledge or a combination of both determines the winning outcome.

The following skills are used in competing:

- Hand-eye coordination
- Reaction time
- Dexterity
- Spatial memory
- Long-term memory
- Pattern recognition
- Organizational skills
- Strategic planning
- Game play knowledge, general knowledge and intelligence.

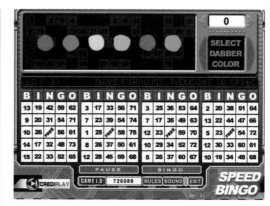

Speed Bingo is a version of bingo that's based on skill rather than chance.

Of course, there are also games in which players go head to head. One example is pool (Snooker). No different than going into a pub to play some 8 ball, you enter a virtual lobby and choose a prize pool. For example, it may cost you 25 cents to play and another $5 goes into the prize pool. Or you may decide on a lesser prize pool of $1. Either way, you pay the house a fee to play.

When you challenge another player, each of you pays the fee to the "house," and each of you contributes toward the predetermined prize pool. Then you play, and the winner takes the prize pool.

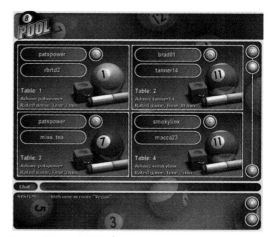

The pool lobby at SkillArcade.com is much less smoky than what you'd find in a bricks-and-mortar pool hall.

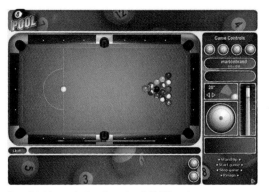

A pool table, racked and ready, at SkillArcade.com.

How to Play Games

First you choose your site and go through the registration process. (You have to register even if you want to play for free.) After registering, you receive your free cash credits. You can use the cash credits to participate in free tournaments against other free-tournament players. Redeeming the cash credits for real cash and participation in larger, cash prize tournaments requires a credit card deposit.

Not unlike free games at online casinos, free skill tournaments are designed to get new users comfortable with how larger cash prize tournaments work. And many sites will only let you play a number of games for free before making you deposit money or upgrade to

A sample online account from SkillArcade.com.

unlimited free games membership.

Once you have mastered a game and want to play for cash, it works something like this:

You log in to your account and go to the deposit section. A credit card, PayPal or NETeller account is used to purchase credits. The sites generally ask that you deposit a minimum of $20, although larger amounts of credits can be purchased. The site operators need to do this because they usually absorb the cost of processing charged by the bank.

You are now a cash gamer using credits to play in tournaments for cash. Now you want to play a tournament of skill, so it's time to choose a game to play.

During the setup of the game, it might be necessary to downloaded software. The software is integral to play the games and does not interfere with your operating systems. Typically, it's an add-on from Macromedia, which enables installation of the shockwave player. And make sure you allow pop-ups on your browser!

The entrance fee and the prize pool contribution are posted along with the minimum number of players and a time limit on the tournament. You then opt to play the tournament and the fees are debited from your account. If you win the tournament, your account is credited with the total amount of the prize pool from the tournament.

As mentioned, the entrance fee is sort of like a golf course greens fee. It enables the skill games company to have the prize pool contribution, which is just like a prize pool for any golf tournament. The provider of the games does not profit from the size of a player's wager on his or her own skills. In fact, players don't "wager" at all; they simply decide how big of a prize pool they want to enter and they play the games. The provider doesn't profit from the size of the cash prize pool either. Nor does it profit if one player wins over another specific player. To ensure that the provider is running games of skill and not gambling sites, determinations are made by gaming experts and legal counsel.

Tournaments generally run no longer than five minutes and involve five people on average. Thousands of tournaments can be played per day depending on the number of users on the system.

If you have lots of wins and wish to withdraw the cash, you go to the withdraw section and a check is sent

After all games are completed, the game results page at SkillArcade.com shows you whether you've won any money, and if so, how much.

to you (usually within five days). If you use PayPal or NETeller, your account is credited automatically.

When you win, your account is immediately updated and shows a credit. You typically don't see whether you've won until all your opponents have already played.

Good news arrives via email from SkillArcade.com.

Many sites even e-mail you a notification of who won the tournament so you don't have to keep checking your account.

Playing to Win—How to Improve Your Skills

Skill games not only provide you with a chance to win money, they also provide you with good entertainment value. You probably won't win as much money as you might if you hit the jackpot on a casino site, but there is money to be made.

Providers try to match users with similar skills to level the competition, though players often also have the option to compete with whomever they want. There are also usually free practice games at an easy level, which you can enter in order to become familiar with the rules and interface before engaging in a cash competition. So, use the free credits and play as many games for free as you can before you play for cash.

And which game should you play? No one game gives you any better chances over another one because you are playing against other people's skill sets. The best thing to do is play all the games available on the site and choose the one in which you excel the most. Then hone your skills and get ready to compete.

It's a great feeling when you win. Not only have you beaten someone else, but you've been paid for it! And if you lose, you're probably only out a couple of dollars, which is well worth the entertainment value.

What to Look for in a Skill Games Site

Online skill gaming sites are fun and may provide you with hours of entertainment and excitement. Who knows? Maybe you'll win big! When compared with online casinos, there are fewer choices out there right for now. The main ones are hosted in the United Kingdom and USA. Some of the main sites are shown on this page.

Skill Gaming sites are no different from any product out there. Pretend you are booking a hotel online or even buying a car. You shop around. When you look for an online skill games site, consider the following:

Samples game at SkillArcade.com: Skeet Shoot.

Samples of games at SkillArcade.com: Munch Man.

Unlike online casinos, skill gaming sites do not need to be licensed. Look for sites that are owned by companies that are publicly listed or have outside auditors listed on their site. Playing at a site operated by a company that has to adhere to the Securities and Exchange Commission provides a good sense of security.

Most sites accept all major credit cards, NETeller and/or PayPal. Some also allow you to transfer money directly from your bank account.

The better sites will post some sort of fair ranking scheme so that players are matched with worthy opponents. This is important because as you start, you won't be as good as someone who has been playing for months or even years. This will give you a better chance at winning.

SkillArcade.com (North America).

SkillJam (North America).

WorldWinner (North America).

MidasPlayer (United Kingdom).

MiniClip (United Kingdom).

Contact their customer service and ask some questions. You can usually tell a lot about a company by contacting it first and asking them why you should play there instead of somewhere else. Ask them how fast they pay out winnings.

Don't get suckered into a bonus. Read the fine print. And remember, you don't get something for nothing in this world… You wouldn't walk into the Bellagio or Caesars, put $100 on a blackjack hand, call over the pit boss, and demand a $20 bonus!

Do a test. Deposit some money. Play some games and then ask to withdraw your balance. See how fast it comes and how much they charge for withdrawals. Is it fair?

Try the games. Do they download quickly? Do they freeze up when you play? Do you like playing them?

Skill Gaming is an enjoyable pastime, so most of all, look for a site that offers good entertainment value for your money!

A live example— SkillArcade.com

Each user in the system is assigned a skill rating for each game based upon his or her past performance in that game.

To start the user is assigned a skill rating of 1600 which is a beginner rating. He will maintain this rating for the first 20 games of play, at which time he will be assigned a new rating based on the following method.

Each time a player wins a game, his rating will increase based upon the rank of the player or players that he defeated. If the rating of the opponents is much higher than the player, the rating will increase by more than if his opponents had the same rating or less. When the player loses a game, his rating will drop, the amount of which is also determined by the opponents rating.

For example, Joe is assigned a rating of 1600 for Darts. He wins one game and loses one game against a player with a 1900 rating. The result might look like the following:

- Initital Rating: 1600
- After 1st Game: 1875
- After 2nd Game: 1850

His rating still remains high, as he did manage a win against strong opposition. Should he have lost to a player with a 1500 rating on his second game, his rating would have dropped far more dramatically.

TELEVISION AND MOBILE GAMBLING

This section covers some more
modern forms of gambling, those
on our smaller screens.

INTERACTIVE TELEVISION GAMBLING

Digital television networks were introduced to consumers in the late 1990s. In addition to clearer pictures, better audio, and a larger number of channels, digital TV also enabled broadcasters to provide two-way interactive services. Now viewers can vote for their favorite competitors in reality TV shows and competitions, participate in opinion polls and to switch to different camera angles while watching a football game—all through a television interface. At the push of a button, viewers can also access a broad menu of other content and services, including shopping, quiz games, puzzle games, action/adventure games, and of course, betting games.

Requirements/Technology

Most digital TV networks require subscribers to have set-top boxes. This device enables a television to receive and decode digital broadcasts. It also stores the software and other necessary systems that enable the television to display the user interface that the viewer will use to navigate through the network's interactive menus.

Set-top boxes communicate with digital networks via

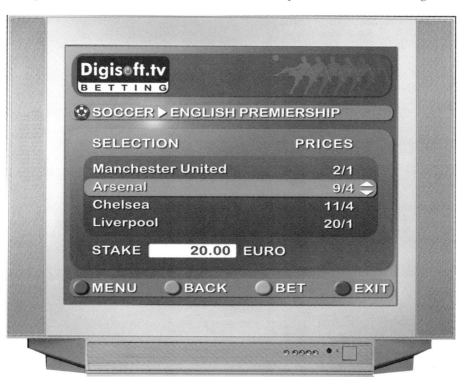

The Digisoft front end offers simple menu choices.

satellite, cable, and terrestrial lines. It is, therefore, necessary that the set-top be connected to both a television and the means of communication. For example, a set-top box that communicates with a digital satellite network, such as Sky digital in the United Kingdom, must have a mini-dish unit installed and must also be connected to a phone line in order to use interactive services. Broadband networks like Telewest and NTL access the digital networks through a direct cable connection.

At the moment, the UK's digital television networks offer viewers the world's most advanced interactive capabilities. It is estimated that about 15 million households in the United Kingdom are equipped to access interactive television services through the country's four digital networks—Sky digital, Telewest Broadband, NTL and iTV digital. The Sky network took a daring step in encouraging the switch to digital

networks in 1999 by offering free set-top-boxes and mini-dishes to customers, and the equipment has remained inexpensive since then. Set-top-boxes are upgraded with new technology on a fairly frequent basis, but overall interactive services development occurs at a slower rate because few homes upgrade their equipment as soon as new models are released. Service providers must try to accommodate the lowest common denominator to insure that the widest range of customers can access their offerings, rather than catering to only those with the newest state of the art machines.

Accessing interactive services through digital television is as easy as pushing a button on the television's remote control. Many channels have their own interactive portals that can be accessed at any time while watching a broadcast. For example, pressing the red button while on a BBC channel will cause the BBC's own unique interactive menu services to pop up. The

The Sky Active digital TV portal.

broadcast will be reduced to a quarter of the full screen size and moved to one corner of the screen so that the viewer may continue to see and hear the programming. A completely different interactive menu would pop up if the viewer pressed the red button while he was on a Sky channel. In this case the Sky Active portal pops up and pushes the broadcast off to a corner of the screen.

The Interactive TV Betting Experience

Interactive betting services through interactive television allow players to bet on the action they are watching by simply pressing a button on their remote control. The experience of betting on interactive television is, therefore, very different from the Internet betting experience. A person who places a bet over the

Choose the action you wish to follow... (Sky Sports Active).

Internet usually has a clear purpose in mind when he logs into his betting account and browses through the betting options. On the other hand, much betting done via interactive television is done on an impulsive whim. Imagine someone sitting at home flipping through the channels and eventually finding a game of keno that is being hosted by a special celebrity guest who happens to be her favorite movie star. She might just be inclined to participate in the next number drawing since it would be as easy as pressing a button. Or imagine a dedicated Manchester United fan who has just watched his team score two goals in seven minutes to shorten the other team's lead to just one goal. In his excitement, the fan might be so confident that Man U will score again that

he would wager on it, and he could do so without missing a single second of the action just by pressing the red button on his remote control. In both situations the simplicity of placing a bet via interactive television has probably played a large role in the person's decision to participate. Perhaps neither viewer would have placed a bet if it were necessary for them to go through the hassle of logging on to the Internet and then accessing a particular Web site before they could execute the bet.

What Kind of Betting is Available?

The most innovative uses of interactive television for betting involve the broadcast of events on which viewers can wager. For example Avago, on channel 181 of the Sky digital network, features live broadcasts of keno-like numbers games in which a presenter pulls numbered balls from a machine and viewers at home mark the numbers off of their play cards as they are called. In order to play a game of Avago Balls, viewers must purchase one or more virtual cards. The cards are then displayed on the viewer's television screen as the game commences. Called numbers are automatically marked off of players' cards and players are automatically notified when they win. A game of Avago Balls lasts only a few minutes.

Sky Bet Live, Channel 295 on the Sky digital network, broadcasts keno games like Super Keno, Turbo Draw and Super 7s that function much the same way as Avago. The channel has a regular schedule of live broadcast programming that is entirely devoted to betting. Among its most exciting offerings is virtual horse and dog racing. Viewers are shown the odds for each computerized dog or horse running in the upcoming race and can place a wager on a number of options, including whether a particular animal will place or show. Race results are determined by a random number generator, and the racing is accompanied by live commentary by experienced pundits.

It is, of course, possible to wager on actual horse and dog races as well. At The Races—channel 415 on the Sky digital network—is devoted entirely to horse racing, featuring live racing broadcasts as well as news, results, commentaries, analysis, and betting tips. The channel has partnered with 28 British racecourses and provides live racing coverage and betting for races at those courses plus 27 Irish and four American racecourses. Pressing the red interactive button while watching At The Races shrinks the broadcast to one a quarter size of the screen and brings up the channel's interactive menu, allowing punters to continue to watch and listen to the broadcast as they browse through the wagering odds. At The Races has several betting partners (Blue Square, Totesport, Littlewoods Bet Direct, Ladbrokes and Skybet), all of whose odds punters can browse through before making a final decision on their wager.

The same is true for other sporting events; viewers can place bets while they continue to watch the action in one corner of the screen. The viewer simply presses the interactive button to bring up a menu that allows him to browse the sporting odds from all of the channel's betting partners.

One of the newest developments in interactive television is in-running-betting. With in-running-betting, punters can place a wager on what sort of action will happen next within a sports competition. For example, with in-running-betting on football matches a punter could wager on which team or player will score the next game, which player will receive the next card and which player will get the next throw-in. This sort of play-by-play betting is available for most major British sports, including football, cricket, golf, rugby, tennis and snooker. The concept of in-running-betting is one that especially lends itself to impulse betting. No longer does a punter have to settle for betting on the overall result of the game; now he can wager on a number of occurrences within the game. In-running-betting even gives punters who have lost on the final outcome of the game a chance to regain some of their stake by correctly predicting what sort of play will occur next.

Fixed-odds casino gaming is another popular interactive service on digital networks. At the moment all casino gaming services must be accessed through an interactive portal (such as Sky Active on the Sky digital network), and there is no interaction with a live audio-video broadcast. Sky digital viewers can press the interactive button at anytime to access the Sky Active portal. Once there, they can navigate through the easy-to-use interactive services interface to find and select the "Puzzles & Jackpots" section. From within this section, players can access the games offered by providers like

Fancy a Flutter, PlayMonteCarlo, Littlewoods Game On and Sky Bet Vegas. Each site offers its own distinct variety of number games, dice games, roulette, slots, bingo and hi-lo.

The William Hill TV channel (425 on Sky), for example, offers 10 interactive numbers games that may be accessed around the clock by pressing the red button, including King Keno, Roll' Em Dice, Trackside virtual horse racing, roulette, Hi-Lo, two spin-the-wheel games and three slots games. William Hill TV also features live greyhound racing for Brough Park and exclusive US horse racing.

The UK National Lottery makes some of its products available over the Sky digital network via the Sky Active menu. Players can participate in both the Lotto and Euromillions and can purchase up to eight weeks of tickets at a time. The National Lottery automatically checks the numbers for players and notify them if they are lucky enough to have won.

The interactive fixed-odds casino games offered via interactive television are, however, much more limited in their offerings compared to their Internet counterparts because of technological limitations and legal restrictions. Interactive gaming services over digital television networks are not as visually stunning as their Internet counterparts due to the slow speed of communication between the server and the set-top box and also to the relative newness of the technology. While Internet casinos can communicate at high-speed broadband rates, digital television connections are limited to the speed of dial-up modem connections. It is, therefore, necessary to keep the amount of information that must be transmitted back and forth between the set-top-box and the central server at a minimum. Set-top-box technology is also a relatively new development compared to the PC, and the units have slower microprocessors and less random access memory. As a result, the games are not as rich and dynamic as those that can played on a standard PC over the Internet. But there is no doubt that as new models of set-top-boxes are developed they will continue to become faster and better equipped to store and run rich games.

Interactive television services like PlayMonteCarlo, Sky Bet Vegas and William Hill TV are also limited in what sorts of games they may offer behind the red button because of regulatory restrictions. Games like blackjack and video poker are prohibited from digital television networks in the United Kingdom because they are classified separately from games like keno and roulette, which are classified as fixed-odds games. UK law does not allow interactive gambling operators to provide games of chance, although sports betting and fixed-odds betting are acceptable. Companies like Ladbrokes and William Hill can offer games of chance to British residents over the Internet because they have based their computer servers in offshore jurisdictions that license online gambling. British law acknowledges that the gambling activity takes place wherever the gambling provider's server is located, so it is, therefore, not illegal for Ladbrokes to offer games of chance over the Internet. Companies cannot offer games of chance over the digital television networks because a server based offshore cannot efficiently communicate with a UK-based digital television network.

Proposed legislation in the British Parliament would update the country's gambling policies. Among other changes proposed are measures that would permit a Gambling Commission to issue interactive gaming licenses (including for games of chance) to companies, which would likely bring many of the offshore servers back to the United Kingdom. However, the Bill has met much opposition, and at the moment there is no certainty as to whether or not it will pass.

Accounts

Bettors can usually use the same wagering account across all of a gambling provider's interactive services. For example, a customer of William Hill can register a single credit card with the company and then use that account to pay for betting across William Hill's Internet, mobile and interactive television wagering services. It is not possible to have betting expenses added to one's digital television bill. And while it's possible to set up an account over the TV, it's not practical because the remote controls don't provide letter pads. It is, therefore, much easier to register over the Internet.

Global Perspective

At the moment, the United Kingdom has by far the most robust interactive television betting services in the world. Not only is the United Kingdom home to some of the most advanced digital television networks with some of the finest interactive offerings all across the board, but it also happens to be the only country with such well developed interactive digital television systems that also has a liberal approach to gambling. The digital networks in Australia, Hong Kong, Japan and the United States will likely catch up to the United Kingdom quickly with respect to interactive television capabilities, but they are not likely to begin offering gambling services through the television any time in the near future.

MOBILE GAMBLING

The first cellular phone call was made in 1977. At the time, the purpose of the new invention was simply to have a device that could make and receive telephone calls from any place at any time. Now over 80% of adults in most European countries (and close to 100 percent of adults in some countries, like Greece, Hong Kong and Taiwan) possess a mobile phone that can not only send and receive phone calls but also provide a number of multimedia features. Equipped with the right technology, a modern cell phone or other mobile device can connect to the Internet and carry streaming audio and video. At the moment, ringtones, instant messaging, and skill games are really the only mobile offerings that have attained wide popularity. This is due mostly to the relative newness of mobile phone applications, the public's unfamiliarity with their capabilities, and the broad range of different cellular networks and enabling technologies.

Common Terms and Technology

Although the world's most advanced mobile phones are capable of remaining connected to the Internet at all times, many individuals either lack the most modern equipment to remain "always on" or are not subscribed to cellular carriers that operate over the most advanced networks. The current top-of-the-line devices that are always on—or always connected to the Internet—use what is referred to as third generation (3G) communication networks. However, second generation (2G) networks, which are much more limited in capabilities, are still predominant in most parts of the world.

Personal digital assistants (PDAs) and other devices are also capable of accessing mobile networks, and it is therefore worth noting that what is true for mobile phones in the discussions below is also true for these devices.

2G Networks

GSM refers the most common cellular communications network, in use in over 200 countries. This type of network was given the name Groupe Special Mobile during a European Telecommunications conference in 1982 at which delegates decided to develop a pan-European mobile communications network. It was not until 1991, however, that the first GSM network was deployed.

CDMA (Code Division Multiple Access) is another type of 2G network that is abundant around the globe,

particularly in North and South America. CDMA and GSM networks are quite evenly comparable in many regards concerning the deployment of multimedia applications and broadband access.

At the beginning of 2004, there were an estimated 1.34 billion cellular customers around the world. An overwhelming majority of those users—72 percent—were on 2G or 2.5G networks.

WAP Technology

WAP (Wireless Application Protocol) technology was created as a means of enabling mobile phones to connect to the Internet by using 2G cellular networks. WAP provides a language that allows Web developers to create web pages that can be displayed on the small display screens of most mobile phones. WAP-enabled phones can therefore access the Internet, but the experience is hardly comparable to that of the World Wide Web, where Web surfers use browsers to access literally millions of Web pages. Conversely, mobile phone users who rely on WAP technology can only view sites that were composed in WAP.

To access the Internet via a WAP-enabled device on a 2G network, a user must access a dial-up connection that is not only slow (21 kbps per second) but also susceptible to frequent disconnections. Although it is not very common anymore, many 2G operators at first only allowed subscribers to access content that was available at their closed portals, which compared to the Internet, provided an extremely narrow amount of material. 2G subscribers who can access content outside of the cellular operator's portal sometimes find the process of actually reaching the destination site tedious. To reach a site outside the portal requires the user to manually enter every letter of the site's URL. For example, an individual trying to reach a site at http://mobile.sportsbook.com/betnow (a fictional site) would have to type in every letter of the address through his number pad. Although some people still find the process of typing on tiny numbered pads a hassle, many have grown accustomed to it. There are even competitions to see who can type fastest on numbered pads.

A final hindrance to WAP-enabled browsing is that it is difficult to ensure that a WAP Web site's layout and presentation will remain consistent across several different browsing devices.

2.5G Networks

The year 2000 saw the introduction of GPRS (General Packet Radio Service), an addition to 2G networks that enabled mobile phones to not only be always connected to the network, but also to provide for connection speeds that reach as high as 56kbps. While 2G services must charge users a fee for accessing Internet-based material that is based upon the length of a dial-up call, 2.5G services are able to charge users on a per-packet basis, ensuring that the user pays only for the bandwidth he uses. GPRS is therefore well suited to e-mail and other non-bandwidth intensive tasks.

An alternative form of 2.5G technology is the i-mode system developed by Japanese operator NTT DoCoMo. i-mode differs from GPRS and WAP systems in that it uses a compact version of the HTML Web language. The language resembles standard HTML so much that Web developers can quickly and easily create new Web sites without having to learn the completely new language used by WAP sites.

GPRS is commonly referred to as 2.5G technology because it is considered a sort of transition in technology between 2G and the next major improvement: 3G.

3G Networks

3G networks have made high-speed data connections over mobile devices a reality, and are thought to be the final chain in the process that should lead to the take off of online mobile Internet browsing and services. With 3G, mobile surfers are no longer limited to plain-looking sites that were built with mobile specific technologies like WAP; now they can view HTML and XHTML Web pages and enjoy an experience that closely resembles surfing the Internet from a home PC.

Java and J2ME

The creation of the Java programming language in 1995 by Sun Microsystems provided a way for a program or Web site to be written on one PC and then downloaded by another that would be able to run the program just as well. J2ME (Java 2 Platform Micro Edition) was spawned from Java in 1999 and is today the most common platform for mobile gambling games. Mobile program developers use J2ME to create mobile casino games that are compatible with all Java-enabled handsets. Java games can be rich in color, graphics, sound and animation, although they can seem primitive when compared to the amazing dynamics of some of the latest Internet-based casinos.

SMS and MMS

Most people know SMS (Short Message Services) as mobile text messages. A mobile phone user can use the number keys to type a message and then send it to a friend or coworker who will receive the message on his phone almost simultaneously. Most cellular operators charge either a monthly fee or a per-message fee to use SMS, so it is usually necessary for the user to have the cellular provider activate Short Message Servicing capabilities on the phone when he enters a new cellular contract. Most 2G, 2.5G and 3G phones should be equipped to send and receive text messages.

Multimedia Messaging Services (MMS) technology allows SMS messages to be embedded with feature-rich multimedia, like pictures, sounds, animation and even video. They can be used over 2G, 2.5G and 3G networks and support data in GIF, JPEG, MPEG4, MP3, MIDI and WAV file formats.

One of the most common ways to download Java-based games and applications is through the transmission of MMS messages. Typically the instructions for downloading a mobile game command the user to send a text message to a certain number. Soon afterward the user will receive a return MMS message from the mobile site's server. Usually contained in the MMS message is the program that will be automatically downloaded onto the user's phone for use at any time. Alternatively, sometimes the return message will redirect users to another mobile site to download the program. Some companies do not use text messages to transmit applications; the instead simply direct users to the address where they can download the software.

The Mobile Gaming Experience

Throughout much of the world, the cellular phone has become an essential accessory for the contemporary man and woman. Cellular subscription rates have grown so inexpensive that now almost everyone can afford instant remote communication with anyone, anywhere at anytime.

The most notable aspect about gambling over the mobile phone is the ease and convenience with which it can be done. Just as a phone call can be placed from anywhere at anytime via a mobile device, so can a wager. A punter who is itching to place a bet on the big game no longer must wait until he can log onto the Internet stroll down to nearest betting shop. Now he can place the very same wager just by pulling the phone from his pocket and pressing a few buttons.

Not only does the mobile phone offer a great convenience to the modern gambler, but it also provides a great way to stay occupied during the downtime while commuting on a bus or train. A punter who has a twenty minute train ride to and from work each day can keep entertained with a few hands of blackjack. Or, if he's a sports fan he could scour the bookies' sites in order to find a great wagering value.

The introduction of in-running-betting and play-by-play betting has also fostered a great use for wagering on the mobile phone. Now punters can even place a bet as they sit at the stadium watching the game. At the press of a few buttons a player in the stands can take a gamble on whether a penalty kick will be successful. Or he could place a wager on which team or which player will score the next goal. He can even place a quick wager if he's sitting in a pub watching the game on TV with some friends.

There are, of course, a few drawbacks to betting via the mobile phone as compared to over the Internet. First of all, the mobile phone screen is very small, and most devices are not capable of displaying the rich graphics many people have come to expect from the Internet. The punter's experience is also likely to be hindered if he connects via a 2G network, which makes him susceptible to slow speeds, dropped connections, and high usage fees.

Types of Gambling

Many Internet betting companies have begun rolling out mobile versions of casino games. The first mobile casinos games began appearing in 2001, but because they utilized WAP technology over 2G networks, they were very basic with little animation and low-resolution graphics. The spread of 2.5G and 3G networks as well as the development of more advanced mobile phones has fostered great improvement as far as mobile casino games are concerned. Mobile games of roulette, craps, blackjack, video poker, baccarat, keno, slot machines, plus more now exist at various mobile casinos. Although the new versions of mobile casino games are superior to their 2G predecessors, there is still much room for improvement. Most mobile casinos have very few games to offer, and the games are still graphically lacking compared to even the most basic Internet offerings. Nevertheless, the gambling is still very real and enjoyable. Several of the world's most popular Internet gambling sites already offer casino games for play over mobile phones, including Ladbrokes (wap.ladbrokes.com), William Hill (wap.willhill.com), Golden Palace (www.goldenpalacemobile.com) and Paddy Power (wap.paddypower.com).

Perhaps the most practical application of mobile betting services over mobile networks has been the implementation of mobile lotteries. As very simple numbers games, lotteries do not require rich animation or colorful graphics. Lottery services are therefore easy to play and use over most mobile phone networks. With mobile lotteries players can purchase tickets to lottery drawings any time they wish without having to travel to the nearest vendor. Players can choose their own numbers or have them chosen automatically for weekly drawings, or they could even spend a few minutes playing mobile versions of instant scratch tickets. The UK National Lottery's mobile service already enables players to participate in draw-based lottery games via text messaging, while another British lottery, Mlotto (www.mlotto.co.uk) has also created a mobile presence. Globally, mobile lotteries exist for players in Latvia, South Korea, the Netherlands, India, China, Sweden, and in many more countries.

Sports betting systems have had a much easier time converting to the mobile phone platform than have casino games. The nature of sports betting is such that heavy graphics and animation are not necessary. The only data that needs to be displayed for sports betting programs is text-based information, which even 2G networks have no problems transmitting. Most sports betting sites use WAP technology because there is no need for rich graphics. Most sports books also allow punters to access browse through betting information and prices as a guest, even if they have not registered an account with the company. Many of the world's largest Internet bookmakers have expanded their operations to include mobile sports betting platforms, including William Hill, Ladbrokes, Paddy Power, BetWWTS.com (www.betwwts.com) and BetandWin.com (wap.betandwin.com). As stated previously, most of the mobile bookmakers have either added or are in the process of adding in-running-betting and play-by-play betting options.

Even punters who prefer to place their bets with betting exchanges instead of with the traditional bookmakers can access the bets they desire over a mobile phone network. A downloadable program called Mobex provides a mobile interface the Betfair betting exchange network. Mobex is fully transactional and allows users to back and lay competitors on the full range of markets using their regular Betfair accounts. The program is fast, secure, and easy to use but is available only on a subscription-basis of £7.50 per month to users who wish to place bets through the service. Customers who only wish to use the program as a way to view Betfair's prices on the go can access the service the free.

The mobile space is also beginning to see a proliferation of services that provide gambling related information and links to sports books operators. In March 2005 for example, the Racing Post launched a new mobile service that gives users the ability to compare racing and football odds from its sports book partners BlueSquare, Ladbrokes, PaddyPower, SportingOdds and Totalbet. Users can also open and manage accounts with those bookmakers through the Racing Post Mobile service (wap.racingpost.uk).

Many mobile software providers have begun releasing downloadable games of Texas Hold 'Em, the massively popular social poker game, but nearly all of them pit the player against computerized opponents, and playing for real money is not an option. At the time of this book's publication, however, one of the Internet's most successful poker networks, PokerRoom.com, was about to launch a mobile poker application that would enable players to compete against one another for real money.

Generally, most mobile betting services have self-explanatory, very easy-to-use interfaces. From the main screen, punters usually have the option to login, open an account, or enter as a guest. Some sites may permit a new customer to register an account by texting their personal information on the mobile phone, but it is far easier to either set up an account through the company's web site or by calling customer service. Almost every betting company allows customers to use the same credit card account to access services at betting shops, over the Internet and via interactive television and mobile phone.

The Future

It is time to brace yourself for an explosion of brilliant mobile gambling opportunities. Phones that can process and display highly complex information already exist, as do large networks that can transmit data at secure high speeds and remain always connected to the Internet.

Such services are only lagging at the moment because there are various competing networks and technologies all over the globe that are not entirely compatible with another. In the very near future, as more and more carriers upgrade to 3G services, the possibilities will truly be endless.

APPENDIX

APPENDIX I: LEGAL AND JURISDICTIONAL ISSUES

The legality of Internet gambling in many places is anything but clear. As stated in other sections of this book, the authors and publishers make no assumptions regarding the laws in the jurisdiction where the reader is located. Obviously, whether online gambling is legal depends on where you're located, and this is often difficult to determine because most jurisdictions don't have laws in the books pertaining specifically to Internet gambling activity. Another reason for the murkiness from the player's perspective is that most laws pertaining to Internet gambling concern the legality of operating a gambling business as opposed to participating as a casual gambler. Therefore, much of this section will concentrate on the activity of gambling businesses. The purpose of including it is to educate the reader on how gambling sites are regulated and to what degree sites are held accountable for their actions depending on where they're located. In short, it would

ALDERNEY GAMBLING CONTROL COMMISSION

AGCC	Applications	Documentation	Licensees	Players	News	Contact Us	Links
Electronic Betting Centre		Interactive Gaming Licensees		Certificate of Prior Approval		Bookmakers	Objections

Interactive Gaming Licensees

Licence No.	Company Name	Website
001	Ritz Interactive Ltd	www.theritzclublondon.com
004	Bonne Terre Ltd	www.skybetvegas.com
005	Cryptologic Alderney Ltd	
007	Rank Interactive Gaming (Alderney) Ltd	www.hardrockcasino.com
008	Harrah's Online Ltd	
010	Wagerworks (Alderney) 2 Ltd	www.gamesxtra.co.uk
012	Wagerworks (Alderney) 4 Ltd	www.thepriceisrightgames.com
013	Blue Square Gaming (Alderney) Ltd	www.bluesqcasino.com
014	Wagerworks (Alderney) 5 Ltd	www.virgingames.com
015	Cantor Casino (Alderney) Ltd	
016	Paddy Power (Alderney) Ltd	www.paddypowercasino.com
017	Wagerworks (Alderney) 3 Ltd	

The Alderney Gambling Control Commission lists all of its interactive gambling licensees on its Web site.

be nice to know whether the gambling sites that you patronize are operating legally and under close supervision of regulatory authorities, and this is a brief guide for doing just that.

Jurisdictions

Following is a list of online gambling jurisdictions. Much of the information in this section is drawn from IGamingNews.com. It's strongly advisable that you gamble with a site that's government-licensed and regulated. When you're visiting an online gambling site, always check for a notice of license. But beware: Some sites claim to hold a government license when in actuality they don't. The only way to distinguish the legitimate licensees from the imposters is to look them up at the licensing body's Web site. Several jurisdictions keep updated lists of licensed online gambling sites. Some of them even post lists of licensees and/or former licensees that aren't in good standing.

⊛ ALDERNEY – Alderney is a self-governing, British off-shore tax alternative to larger jurisdictions. Its online gambling regulations are strict, and it has attracted some of the world's top gambling providers. It offers licenses to sports betting, race betting and casino operators, and recently removed a restriction forbidding its licensees from welcoming US bettors.

⊛ Alderney Gambling Control Commission: www.gamblingcontrol.org

⊛ ANJOUAN – This country (an island nation east of Africa) began hosting Internet gambling operations. The degree to which those sites are regulated is questionable.

⊛ ANTIGUA & BARBUDA – The Caribbean nation of Antigua & Barbuda is one of the world's oldest online gambling jurisdictions. Its Internet gambling license covers all types of gambling. Some of its licensees have been operating for nearly a decade. The country has a defined set of regulations by which licensees must abide, however, its criteria for obtaining an online gambling license doesn't match that of "top-tier" jurisdictions.

⊛ Antigua & Barbuda Directorate of Offshore Gaming: www.dirgaming.gov.ag

⊛ AUSTRALIA – Several states in Australia allow corporate bookmakers and state-licensed betting agencies to offer race betting and sports betting online. There is also one online casino, Lasseters.com, operating out of Australia's Northern territory. It is interesting to note the Lasseters is allowed to take play from customers located anywhere in the world except Australia. Gambling sites licensed in Australia must comply with very stringent regulations and are generally a safe choice for consumers looking for a high level of player protection. Following are links to the Web sites of Australia's state gambling regulators.

⊛ ACT Gambling & Racing Commission: www.gamblingandracing.act.gov.au

⊛ New South Wales Department of Gaming and Racing: www.dgr.nsw.gov.au

⊛ Northern Territory Treasury: www.treasury.nt.gov.au/ntt/licensing

⊛ Queensland Office of Gaming Regulation: www.qogr.qld.gov.au

⊛ Tasmania Treasury: www.treasury.tas.gov.au/domino/dtf/dtf.nsf

⊛ Victorian Casino and Gaming Authority: www.gambling.vcga.vic.gov.au

⊛ Western Australia Department of Racing, Gaming and Liquor: www.orgl.wa.gov.au

⊛ BELIZE – Belize has a free-trade zone that hosts online gambling sites. There are formal regulations to which operators must adhere; however, it is difficult for players to get in direct contact with the regulatory authority because gambling sites are given licenses by master license holders rather than the government itself. Gambling sites licensed in Belize are not allowed to take play from the country's residents.

⊛ CANADA – In 2004, lotteries in British Columbia and Atlantic Canada (collectively: Nova Scotia, New Brunswick, Prince Edward Island and Newfoundland) gained permission to offer their services over the Internet. These are very well regulated sites; however, they are only available to residents of the mentioned provinces. Additionally, Woodbine Entertainment was permitted in 2004 to begin accepting wagers over the Internet on horse racing. In order to play, though, you must register at participating tracks.

⊛ COSTA RICA – Costa Rica is one of the world's oldest online gambling jurisdictions. While it doesn't offer a high level of player protection through regulations, many of its operators are well respected sports books that have been in the online gambling business. Several sports books located in the country belong to an association that has set up standards for online gambling operators.

⊛ CURACAO (NETHERLANDS ANTILLES) – Curacao has hosted several reputable online gambling operations for a number of years. The island has a set of I-gaming regulations that covers all types of gambling. One knock against it is that its gaming licenses are handed out by businesses serving as "master licensees," and is difficult to pinpoint a central gaming authority that's available to consumers with complaints. On the plus side, the Curacao Internet Gaming Association has been established to assure that operators meet certain standards.

⊛ Curacao Internet Gaming Association: http://www.ciga.an

⊛ EUROPE (CONTINENTAL) – Most European member states offer one or more forms of online gambling, but the availability of these sites is limited to residents of the country in which the site is hosted. On exception to this is Liechtenstein, which is home to one of the world's oldest Internet lotteries and invites players from all over the world. Most European gambling sites are generally operated by government-run organizations and most (if not all) of them are very tightly regulated. The following countries in continental Europe have host online gambling operations: Åland Islands (Finland): Austria, Belgium, Denmark, Estonia, Faroe Islands (Realm of Denmark), Finland, France, Germany, Hungary, Iceland*, Ireland*, Liechtenstein, Norway, Scotland*, Slovakia, Spain, and Sweden.

*Iceland, Ireland and Scotland are not part of the main continent, but are included in this group because their regulatory approaches toward online gambling are similar.

⊛ GIBRALTAR – A handful of reputable sports betting services are licensed in Gibraltar.

⊛ HONG KONG – The Hong Kong Jockey Club and the Mark 6 lottery are both offered over the Internet and via mobile devices, but they are only available to Hong Kong residents.

⊛ THE ISLE OF MAN – Located in the center of the British Isles, the Isle of Man is another example of a tightly regulated offshore European jurisdiction. Like Alderney, it is home to a handful of tier-one operators,

and like Alderney, it recently changed its laws to allow US play. The Isle of Man Government Web site: www.gov.im

⊛ ISRAEL – Two online sports books based in Israel made their debuts in 2004. Lotteries and race betting could be permitted in the near future as well. So far, the services have been geared toward only customers in Israel.

⊛ KAHNAWAKE – Kahnawake is a Mohawk Indian nation located just outside Montreal, Quebec. It hosts numerous online gambling services (including some of the world's leading I-gaming Web sites) offering all types of gambling. The nation has a rigid set of regulations and it has a good track record of hosting reputable gambling businesses. It should be noted that the nation is entirely separate from Canada and the province of Quebec.

⊛ Kahnawake Gaming Commission: www.kahnawake.com/gamingcommission

⊛ KALMYKIA (RUSSIA) – Formerly part of the Soviet Union, Kalmykia began offering licensing for Internet gambling in 1999. Little is known about the jurisdiction's regulatory regime or what measures are in place to assure player protection.

⊛ KOREA – Numerous reports indicate that interactive lotteries are being offered in North and South Korea, although neither country's government has made its policy toward Internet gambling clear. It is very difficult to get information in English on these lotteries.

⊛ JAMAICA – The Jamaica Lottery Corporation has been selling its tickets over the Internet since 2001. The tickets are sold all over the world, but U.S. players are off limits. There are also a few Internet sports books operating in Jamaica, although the regulations are relatively loose.

⊛ MALTA – Malta very recently began issuing licensing to online gambling operators for all types of gambling. It hasn't had a chance to build a reputation as a top-tier I-gaming jurisdiction, but as a new member of the European Union, it is likely to only award licenses to companies that are reliable and accountable.

⊛ Malta Financial Services Authority: www.mfsc.com.mt

⊛ MACAU – Customers of the Macau Jockey Club can bet on sporting events via the Internet at: www.macauslot.com.

⊛ MAURITIUS – The Republic of Mauritius, an island

nation in the Indian Ocean, is home to Bowman International Sports, a sports book licensed in Great Britain since 1985. The company launched its online sports betting services in late 2001.

⊛ New Zealand – Only the Lotteries Commission and state-operated sports betting agency are allowed to offer their services over the Internet. Like Australia, New Zealand is a highly regulated jurisdiction.

⊛ New Zealand Department of Internal Affairs: www.dia.govt.nz/diawebsite.nsf

⊛ NICARAGUA – Gambling sites are believed to have begun operating out of Nicaragua in 2000.

⊛ NIGERIA – Subscribers to Nigeria's four mobile phone networks—MTN, Econet, V/Mobile and Global Comm.—can participate in a weekly draw using SMS-compatible cell phones.

⊛ NORFOLK ISLAND (AUSTRALIA) – Norfolk Island is a Pacific territory belonging to Australia. In response to restrictions placed on Internet gambling companies on the continent, Norfolk Island has set up a regulatory regime for online casinos. In terms of player protection, the island's gambling regulations are strict like those of Australia. No online casinos are operating there as of yet.

⊛ Norfolk Island Gaming Authority: www.nlk.nf/gaming

⊛ PANAMA – Gambling sites are believed to have begun operating out of Panama in 2002.

⊛ THE PHILIPPINES – Online gambling sites have been operating out of the Philippines since 2000. Pagcor, a quasi-governmental operation is in charge regulating

GamingNews.com features a running list of jurisdictions that either sanction or allow Internet gambling. Most of the site is only available to subscribers, but the jurisdictions page is open to visitors as well.

Internet gambling sites aimed at citizens in the Philippines, the Cagayan Economic Zone in the northern Philippines grants licenses to Internet gambling operations targeting international customers (but not Philippine residents).

⊛ SOUTH AMERICAN JURISDICTIONS – Several states and countries in South America have enabled their sports betting and/or lottery operators to offer their services online. These services are available only to customers in the jurisdictions where the operators are located. On exception, however, is Margarita Island, a property of Venezuela, where numerous I-gaming sites are reported to be hosted. There are also a few states in Argentina with online gambling services that are available to gamblers all over the world.

⊛ ST. KITTS & NEVIS – The government of St. Kitts and Nevis issues a generic gaming license authorizing the holder to carry on the business of physical gaming, Internet gaming horse or greyhound betting or sports book betting.

⊛ St. Kitts & Nevis Government Web site: www.stkittsnevis.net

⊛ TAIWAN – Customers of Taiwanese lottery operator TaipeiBank can purchase lottery tickets via the Internet using smart cards.

⊛ THE UNITED KINGDOM – By many accounts, the UK is considered the world's hub for online gambling. Most of the country's reputable bookmakers—including world leaders like Ladbrokes and William Hill—offer their services online. These are all very well regulated businesses, many of which have been around for decades. The UK National Lottery also recently began operating online as well. Depending on whether Parliament passes a proposed bill that would overhaul the country's gambling laws, online casinos could begin calling the UK home in the near future too.

⊛ THE UNITED STATES – The only type of online gambling permitted in the United States is race betting. A handful of states—including California, Louisiana and Oregon—host interactive race betting services that are available to customers in a few dozen US states.

⊛ WESTERN CAPE (SOUTH AFRICA) – The Western Cape Gambling & Racing Board has permitted Atlantic SportsBet to operate an online sports book at: www.SportsBet.co.za.

⊛ Gambling & Racing Board Web Site: www.wcgrb.co.za

⊛ VANUATU – This small island in the South Pacific set up a licensing regime for online gambling in 2000. The jurisdictions laws allow for all types of gambling, although the only online gambling sites hosted are sports books. The island's regulations are generally more strict then most "offshore" jurisdictions.

⊛ Vanuatu's Internet Free Trade Zone – www.vanuatugovernment.gov.vu/cyberspace.html

Prohibition

Several jurisdictions have prohibited some or all forms of Internet gambling, including the following:

⊛ AUSTRALIA – Federal law prohibits Australia-licensed online casinos from offering their services to Australian residents. There are also bans on in-running wagers and betting exchanges, although there is some speculation that one or more states will begin sanctioning betting exchanges.

⊛ CHINA – The Chinese government in early 2005 initiated a massive countrywide crackdown on gambling, and Internet gambling activity fell into the scope of the campaign. All forms of gambling (with the exception of state lotteries) are considered illegal in China, but not until recently did authorities begin to consistently target online gambling activity.

⊛ EUROPEAN UNION – Most European member states prohibit foreign gambling companies from offering their services across national borders.

⊛ GREECE – The country of Greece has a law that prohibits all public facilities from offering any form of electronic games—including gambling—to patrons. The intent was to come down on businesses profiting from illegal gambling.

⊛ HONG KONG – While the Hong Kong Jockey Club is allowed to offer its services online to Hong Kong punters, the government strictly prohibits offshore gambling operations from doing the same.

⊛ UNITED STATES – Despite being enacted three decades before the proliferation of the Internet, the Wire Act of 1961 is widely accepted as a ban on Internet sports betting. Applying the law to other forms of gambling, such as lotteries and casino gambling, is a bit of a stretch, and the federal government has been trying to pass a more thorough prohibition bill for the better part of a decade. Meanwhile, a handful of states have laws prohibiting the operation of Internet gambling services.

Self-Regulation

Despite the existence of several jurisdictions that strictly regulate interactive gambling, there are many more with little or no regulations. And there's no presence of any international regulatory body. To fill the void, the industry has done an impressive job of regulating itself. One such means of self-regulation is formation of associations that set standards of the industry and see to it that those standards are met. Three associations, in particular, concentrate their efforts on interactive gambling:

⊛ E-COMMERCE AND ONLINE GAMING REGULATION AND ASSURANCE – eCOGRA's mission, as stated on its Web site is "to be an independent entity that provides important player protections to consumers, including that operators are honest, games are fair, monetary deposits are safe and winning bets are paid in a timely manner." The group awards a Seal of Approval to sites that comply with its standards. Web Site: www.ecogra.com

⊛ INTERACTIVE GAMBLING, GAMING AND BETTING ASSOCIATION – Founded in 2002, iGGBA was created to "address the unique legislative, regulatory and commercial opportunities and concerns of the I-gaming industry." The U.K.-based association states that its aim is "to provide reassurance to playing customers of the probity and trustworthiness of its members, and also to represent the trade, particularly in the formulation and maintenance of formal regulation." Web Site: www.iggba.org.uk

⊛ THE INTERACTIVE GAMING COUNCIL – The IGC is a not-for-profit organization established in 1996 to "provide a forum for interested parties to address issues and advance common interests in the global interactive gaming industry, to establish fair and responsible trade guidelines and practices that enhance consumer confidence in interactive gaming products and services, and to serve as the industry's public policy advocate and information clearinghouse."

Web Site: www.igcouncil.org

APPENDIX II: AVOIDING PRATFALLS

...As a Consumer

Use government-licensed services.

Only play at sites that are government-licensed and regulated. If they claim to be government-licensed, contact the licensing authority (or visit their Web site) to assure that they indeed hold such a license. Also make sure that the license is in good standing.

⊛ LISTEN TO THE PEOPLE

Visit online forums and newsgroups to find out what other players are saying about gambling sites that you're considering. Be aware, however, that overly positive "reviews" are often posted by the sites themselves and that exceptionally slanderous postings often come from competing sites and others with an axe to grind.

⊛ INVESTIGATE

Call online casinos' software suppliers and inquire about the standing of their software licenses. Look the site up at www.whois.org to see if the contact information matches up wit the contact information given on the site.

⊛ LOOK FOR PHONE NUMBERS AND EMAIL ADDRESSES

How easy is the operator to contact? Are their phone numbers and email addresses posted on the site? If so, call them and email them and see how responsive they are. If they aren't easily contacted, stay away.

⊛ TEST CUSTOMER SERVICE

No one wants to patronize any business with poor customer service. Call the customer service number and throw some questions at them. See how they handle it. If you're uncomfortable with the conversation, move on. And if no one responds, or they don't have a customer service number, DEFINITELY move on.

⚙ READ

There are a lot of online and print publications (mentioned throughout this book) that feature reviews and news articles on Internet gambling sites. Sites that are wronging people cannot hide from these publications.

⚙ USE SERVICES THAT BELONG TO INDUSTRY ASSOCIATIONS

Sites located in jurisdictions that don't regulate that strictly aren't necessarily shady operations. Most of them, in fact, are legitimate businesses. One way to verify this is playing at sites that are members of industry associations, such as eGOGRA or the Interactive Gaming Council. Once again, it's always a good idea to make sure they're legitimate members in good standing.

⚙ FAMILIARITY IS IMPORTANT

The online gambling industry is filled with reputable businesses, many of which are recognizable brands. Take advantage of this and play at sites operated by companies with which you're familiar.

⚙ DON'T SWITCH IF IT'S NOT NECESSARY

Many online gamblers like to migrate from site to site because they're always looking for something different, but the more sites you try, the more likely you are to have a negative experience. If you've found a site that you like and trust, and it has everything you're looking for, why not stick with it.

⚙ IF IT SEEMS TOO GOOD TO BE TRUE...

You know the rest. . . "Then it probably isn't." Nothing is free in online gambling. Operators are competing for you business, and they're certainly willing to throw some incentives your way, but if you see a deal that you "can't·pass up," pass it up.

... As a Gambler

⚙ SPEED KILLS

It's great that online casino games move so quickly, but this can be a bad thing too. First of all, you're more likely to make costly errors if you're flying through the game play. Second, your bankroll can disappear in a blink.

⚙ AVOID GIMMICKS

You'll always come across new exciting games (or variations of old games) that look like a lot of fun, but 99 times out of 100, they offer very poor odds. If you think you've found the exception, do some research before playing. It's a guarantee that the odds gurus have gotten their hands on it.

⚙ USE CHEAT SHEETS

Your chances of winning at games like video poker and blackjack are greatly improved when you use perfect strategy. Unless you've got every proper move memorized, use a cheat sheet. You're cheating yourself if you don't

⚙ PAY ATTENTION

Gambling online is nice because you can watch TV, press a shirt, talk on the phone or do whatever else your heart desires as you play, but don't let distractions detract from your decision making process, especially when it comes to money management and playing games that require skill. The same goes for chatting online with other players.

... As a Responsible Individual

⚙ SET LIMITS

Before you play, establish maximum amounts of time and money you're willing to spend and do not stray from your limits.

⚙ WALK AWAY

Step away from the computer. Even if you're not losing your shirt, it's always a good idea to get away from the games an clear your head.

⚙ DON'T PLAY

If you have pre-existing gambling problem, or you think you might have one, then don't gamble on the Internet.

APPENDIX III: KNOW WHEN TO STOP

The authors of this book collectively and individually recognize the importance of gambling responsibly and urge anyone who gambles to be aware of the dangers of compulsive gambling. Gambling should be a form of entertainment and not a cause of stress, debt, family problems and other misfortunes. This appendix lists a few very helpful resources that should a) help the reader recognize the signs when gambling becomes a problem; and b) provide avenues for recovery.

Following are some very basic tips for keeping your gambling under control:

⦿ SET LIMITS. Predetermine a maximum amount of time and a maximum amount of money you will spend, and stick to it.

⦿ TAKE BREAKS. Don't immerse yourself in gambling. Periodically walk away from the computer and clear your head.

⦿ CREATE AND "UNTOUCHABLE" FUND. When things are going well, ration a portion of winnings with which your willing to "re-invest" and put the rest away. Do not under any circumstances dip into the untouchable fund.

⦿ CUT YOURSELF OFF. If you're gambling too much, remove all means of instant access to online gambling. Close your accounts and/or uninstall gambling software. This way gambling isn't one click away from your desktop. You might even request to sites at which you've gambled to no longer let you play.

⦿ GET HELP. If you're unable to stop on your own, use the resources listed in this chapter to find a means of support. Enroll in a recovery program.

How Do You Know When You Have a Gambling Problem?

Gamblers Anonymous, an international non-profit organization that provides a 12-step recovery program and support groups for problem gamblers, has developed a set of 20 questions to help individuals determine whether they are compulsive gamblers The organization maintains the most compulsive gamblers will answer yes to seven or more of the questions.

Twenty Questions:

⦿ Did you ever lose time from work or school due to gambling?

⦿ Has gambling ever made your home life unhappy?

⦿ Did gambling affect your reputation?

⦿ Have you ever felt remorse after gambling?

⦿ Did you ever gamble to get money with which to pay debts or otherwise solve financial difficulties?

⦿ Did gambling cause a decrease in your ambition or efficiency?

⦿ After losing did you feel you must return as soon as possible and win back your losses?

⦿ After a win did you have a strong urge to return and win more?

⦿ Did you often gamble until your last dollar was gone?

⦿ Did you ever borrow to finance your gambling?

⦿ Have you ever sold anything to finance gambling?

⦿ Were you reluctant to use "gambling money" for normal expenditures?

⦿ Did gambling make you careless of the welfare of yourself or your family?

⦿ Did you ever gamble longer than you had planned?

⦿ Have you ever gambled to escape worry or trouble?

⦿ Have you ever committed, or considered committing, an illegal act to finance gambling?

⦿ Did gambling cause you to have difficulty in sleeping?

⦿ Do arguments, disappointments or frustrations create within you an urge to gamble?

⦿ Did you ever have an urge to celebrate any good fortune by a few hours of gambling?

⊛ Have you ever considered self-destruction or suicide as a result of your gambling?

SOURCE: www.gamblersanonymous.org

Additional Resources on the Internet

⊛ PROBLEMGAMBLING.COM

www.problemgambling.com – This site offers numerous problem gambling resources, including books and guides as well as phone numbers and addresses for treatment centers.

⊛ THE SAFE GAMING SYSTEM

www.safegamingsystem.com – A comprehensive service that serves as "safety net" to protect gamblers from harm. The system provide an effective, personalized means of maintaining control over your gambling activities by guiding you through decisions about your personal, affordable limits on gambling. Money and time limits are set in advance away from the atmosphere of a gambling venue. Users fund SGS accounts for "budget" periods by pre-purchasing only their affordable limit for gambling, or less.

⊛ GAMBLERS ANONYMOUS INTERNATIONAL DIRECTORY
www.gamblersanonymous.org/mtgdirTOP.html – A list of schedules for and locations of Gamblers Anonymous meetings all over the world.

⊛ PROBLEM GAMBLING LINKS
www.naspl.org/resource.htm – A list of helpful problem gambling links posted at the Web site of the North American Association of State and Provincial Lotteries.

⊛ GAMBLINGFLOOR.COM
www.gamingfloor.com/Problem_Gambling.html— Gaming Floor's problem gambling links page.

APPENDIX IV: RESOURCES ON THE INTERNET

Responsible Gambling

⊛ www.gamblersanonymous.org – If you have a gambling problem (or you suspect you might have a gambling problem) and you want help, Gamblers Anonymous provides the means necessary for getting it.

⊛ www.responsiblegambling.org – The Responsible Gambling Council is a non-profit organization that works for individuals and communities to address gambling in a healthy and responsible way and undertakes public awareness programs designed to prevent gambling-related problems.

Casino Games

⊛ www.TheCrapShooter.com – Duck! Seriously, the Crap Shooter (Larry Edell) is one of the world's top experts on craps, and this is his Web site.

⊛ www.GameMasterOnline – The Game Master is an excellent resource for both online and offline casino gambling. In addition to extensive lessons for learning how to win, the site features tips and secrets about specific online casinos.

⊛ www.StrictlySlots.com – Peruse the archives of the world's top magazine for slots players.

⊛ www.WizardofOdds – If you're wondering how well various casino games pay out, this is the place to go.

Racing

⊛ www.drf.com – DRF Online has more racing and news and information than you can possibly consume.

⊛ www.throroughbredtimes.com – The online version of racing's most popular weekly magazine.

Player's Advocate

⊛ www.CasinoMeister.com – Hands down, the Meister is the world's No. 1 online casino watchdog.

Industry News

⊛ www.IGamingNews.com – Updated news on all aspects of the Internet gambling industry. It's mostly made up of subscriber-only pages, but there are a few valuable bits of free information as well.

⊛ www.OnlineCasinoNews.com – OCN features news articles on important industry developments.

⊛ www.PokerPulse.com – Those who are curious about which online poker sites are seeing the most action can find what they need here.

Poker

⊛ www.pokerstove.com – Software that evaluates the "equity" a hand has in the pot.

⊛ www.twoplustwo.com – An excellent discussion forum dedicated to poker.

⊛ www.wilsonsw.com – Turbo Hold'em training software for Hold'em poker.

Portals/Links Directories

⊛ www.Gambling.com – An optimized search engine for online gambling sites.

⊛ online.CasinoCity.com – This is by far the largest, most comprehensive online gambling links directory on the Internet. Sites are ranked by popularity (according to site usage numbers).

Bingo

⊛ www.BingoVIPClub.com – Access to the latest news, biggest competitions and the best promotions online bingo has to offer.

⊛ www.WhichBingo.com – One of the Web's top bingo links directories.

⊛ www.OnlineBingo.net – A site dedicated entirely to online bingo. In addition to a links directory, it features numerous articles on the world's most popular game.

Free-Play Bingo Sites

⊛ Bingo.com (www.bingo.com)
⊛ Bingo Bugle (www.bingobugle.net)
⊛ Bingo Canada (www.bingocanada.com)
⊛ Gamesville's Bingo Zone (www.bingozone.com)
⊛ LiveFreeBingo (www.livefreebingo.com)
⊛ Bingo Tourney (www.bingotourney.com)

Pay-to-Play Bingo Sites
- ABCBingo (www.abcbingo.co.uk)
- Bingofunland (www.bingofunland.com)
- Bingomania (www.bingomania.com)
- Bingoworks (www.bingoworkz.com)
- Cyber Bingo (www.cyberbingo.com)
- Fun Bingo (www.funbingo.com)
- Party Bingo (www.partybingo.com)
- Ruby Bingo (www.rubybingo.com)
- WOWBingo (www.wowbingo.com)

Directories and Information Sites
- Bingo VIP Club (www.bingovipclub.com)
- CM of the Year (www.cmoftheyear.com)
- Gambling.com (www.gambling.com)
- OnlineBingo.net (www.onlinebingo.net)
- TopBingoSites (www.topbingosites.com)
- WhichBingo (www.whichbingo.com)

Blackjack
- www.bjmath.com – A Web site for those interested in understanding the mathematics behind blackjack strategy.
- www.BlackJackInfo.com – Home of the "Blackjack Strategy Engine," this site shows proper blackjack strategy according to specific game rules.
- www.Conjelco.com/faq/bj.html – A blackjack FAQ page. If you've got questions, they've got answers.
- www.s-a-g-e.com/bjmyths.html – Blackjack myths, facts and playing suggestions.
- www.bj21.com – Stanford Wong's "Blackjack Page." Among several excellent resources is one of the Web's premier blackjack forums.
- www.Blackjack-School.com – The Game Master's complete blackjack school.
- www.SmartGaming.com – Read advice articles from top blackjack player Henry Tamburin.

Mahjong
- The screenshots in the Mahjong chapter are from www.MahjongClub.com and www.DrHo888.com and illustrate the progression of Internet Mahjong.
- The chapter is a surface scan of Mahjong. There's a lot more to the game and you learn more about it at online at sites such as www.mahjongnews.com and www.mahjongmuseum.com. You may also want to read *The Book of Mahjong* by Amy Lo (ISBN 0-8048-3302).

Sports Betting
- www.oddschecker.com – Never mind searching the Web for the best prices at online sports books. This site allows you to compare odds from major online bookmakers.
- www.covers.com – Covers is filled to the brim with helpful information for sports bettors.

Video Poker
- www.SlotCharts.com – This site displays updated jackpot totals for online progressive games. It's particularly helpful for video poker players because it also displays the return rates.
- www.vid-poker.com – A relatively short but sweet list of helpful video poker links.
- www.zamzone.com – Zamzow sells software that helps video poker players perfect their strategy.

Industry Associations
- www.eCOGRA.com – A group that sets standards of Internet gambling operators.
- www.IGamingCouncil.org – A Canada-based association made up of operators and suppliers to the I-gaming industry.
- www.iGGBA.org.uk – A UK-based trade association for operators, technology companies, suppliers of services and other parties directly involved in the I-gaming industry.

APPENDIX V: A–Z OF GAMBLING TERMS

⊛ ACTION – Any kind of wager.

⊛ ALL IN – In poker, if a player runs out of money during a hand, he can play out the hand, but he's excluded from betting in the remaining rounds. When this happens, the player is "all in." The other players continue betting in a side pot, which excludes the all-in player. If the all-in player wins the hand, he gets the money in the original pot, but the money in the side pot goes to the remaining player with the best hand.

⊛ ALLOWANCE RACE – Horses in allowance races must meet certain conditions to run. The amount of weight carried by a horse in such a race is based on the number of races the horse has run and the amount of money it has won.

⊛ AMERICAN WHEEL – A roulette wheel with a total of 38 numbers (0, 00, and numbers 1-36).

⊛ ANTE – When poker players place a small bet into the pot before the hand starts. Antes ensure that at least a small amount of money is invested in the game before everyone can fold.

⊛ BANKROLL – Money available to the person making a bet.

⊛ BASIC/PROPER STRATEGY – using the plays in blackjack that enable you to maximize your chances of winning.

⊛ BIAS – When a horse is more likely to win if it runs on one part of the running surface rather than on another part.

⊛ BINGO CARD – The card used for playing bingo. It contains five rows and five columns of boxes with the letters B I N G O printed across the top. Winning at bingo entails forming required patterns by filling boxes as their corresponding numbers are called.

⊛ Blind Bet – In poker, a blind bet is a bet that selected players are required by the rules to make. It serves the same purpose as an ante.

⊛ BLUFFING – A poker player is bluffing when he bets and raises in an effort to make his opponents believe his hand is better than it really is.

⊛ BRING-IN – A bring-in is when a poker player is forced to get the betting started by opening with a minimal bet. The bring-in bet serves as an ante for seven-card games. It's made after all the players have been dealt their first up-card. The player with the lowest showing card gets the honors. The second bettor can match the bring-in, raise to the minimum bet level or fold.

⊛ BUST – Going over 21 in blackjack. If you bust, you lose.

⊛ BUTTON – This is a small marker in poker that's moved from player to player after each hand to designate the dealer position. The designated dealer position is shifted from hand to hand to ensure that each player is required to take his turns putting up blind bets. The button is moved clockwise around the table after each hand.

⊛ CALLER: The person who calls out the numbers in a bingo game as they are drawn.

⊛ CALLING – In poker, this is when a player matches a previous bet (also referred to as seeing a bet).

⊛ CHALK – The favored team in a sporting event.

⊛ CHECKING – In poker, a player checks when he wants to stay in the game, but doesn't want to bet. You can only check if no one has made a bet during the current round. Once a bet is made, you can call, raise or fold, but you can no longer check.

⊛ CIRCLE GAME – A sporting event with limited action, typically due to key injuries, weather conditions or other factors that make it an unstable play.

⊛ CLAIMING RACE – Horse races typically featuring the least impressive horses and the cheapest purses. Claimers are for sale at races at set prices. The claiming price puts a ceiling on the horses' values, ensuring that the race is evenly matched.

⊛ COLT – An uncastrated male horse aged four or younger.

⊛ COLUMN BET – A roulette bet on any of the

numbers in one of the three roulette table's three columns. (Pays 2–1.)

⊛ COMBINATION BET – Using one or more chips in the same position on a roulette table to bet on more than one number at a time.

⊛ COMBINATION QAY TICKET – a keno ticket in which groups of numbers are bet several different ways.

⊛ COME BET – Betting in craps that the dice will pass, made after the come out roll.

⊛ COME BOX – The area on the craps table layout where come bets are made.

⊛ COME OUT ROLL – The initial or first roll of the dice in craps before any point have been established.

⊛ COMMUNITY CARDS – In poker, community cards are cards that are dealt face up and shared by all players. In Texas Hold'em, for example, each player is dealt two face-down cards and the rest of their hands are composed of five face-up community cards.

⊛ COMPS – Complimentary gifts used by casinos to attract players.

⊛ COPY – When a player and the banker in pai gow poker have the same two-card hand or the same five-card hand. The banker wins all copies.

⊛ CORNER BET – One roulette wager on four numbers at a time. (Pays 8-1.)

⊛ COVER – In sports betting, a team covers by beating the spread by the required number of points.

⊛ COVERALL: A bingo game in which the winner is the first person to fill every box on his card.

⊛ CRAP OUT – To throw a craps on the come out roll; an automatic loser for pass line bettors.

⊛ CRAPS – In craps, this is the term for a roll of a 2, 3 or 12 (along with the name of the game).

⊛ DAILY DOUBLE – A wager in which the bettor selects the winners of two consecutive races, typically the first two races of the day.

⊛ DAUBER – A device used to mark off numbers on a bingo cards as they're called.

⊛ DON'T COME BOX – The area on the craps table layout where don't come bets area made.

⊛ DON'T COME BET – A craps bet made after the come out roll that the dice won't pass; betting against the dice.

⊛ DON'T PASS LINE – The area on the craps table layout where don't pass bets are made.

⊛ DON'T PASS BET – A craps bet made on the come out roll that the dice won't pass; betting against the dice.

⊛ DOUBLE DOWN – In blackjack, this is when you turn your cards face-up, double your bet and receive one and only one more card.

⊛ DOZEN BET – A wager on twelve numbers on the roulette layout at the same time. The numbers are divided as such: 1-12, 13-24, and 25-36.

⊛ DRAW – The second round of cards dealt in draw poker.

⊛ DRAW BUTTON – In video poker, this button allows you to draw up to five new cards.

⊛ DRAW POKER – A poker game in which all cards are dealt face-down.

⊛ EASY WAY – In craps, this is a roll of a 4, 6, 8 or 10 where the dice are not matched as a pair.

⊛ EVEN MONEY – A wager in which neither opponent lays any odds.

⊛ EVEN-ODD BET – A roulette bet that either an even or an odd number will come up. (Pays 1-1.)

⊛ EXACTA – A wager in which the bettor selects the top two finishers in a race (also known as a "perfecta").

⊛ EXPECTED WIN RATE – The percentage of the total amount of money wagered that you can expect to win or lose over time.

⊛ FAST RAIL – A bias in which horses running close to the rail have an edge over those further away from the rail.

⊛ FIELD BET – A craps bet that the next roll of the dice will come up 2, 3, 4, 9, 10, 11 or 12.

⊛ FIFTH STREET   Third round of betting in 7 card stud; the fifth car on the board and the final round of betting in Hold'em poker.

⊛ FILLY – a female horse, four years old or younger.

⊛ FIRST BASE – At the blackjack table, the position on the far left of the dealer, and the first person to be dealt cards.

⊛ FISHING – Staying in poker game longer than you should because your looking for the card that will make your hand a winner.

⊛ FLAT TOP – A slot machine with a fixed jackpot (as opposed to a progressive).

⊛ FLOP – In Texas Hold'em, the second round of betting (following the blinds) starts after the first three community cards are dealt. These three cards are known as the "flop."

⊛ FOLD/FOLDING – In poker, a player folds by

throwing away his cards. After folding, he makes no more bets on that hand, receives no more cards during the hand and cannot win the pot.

⊛ FOURTH STREET – The second round of betting in 7 card stud (each player has four cards); the fourth card on the board in Hold'em poker and the third round of betting.

⊛ FRENCH/EUROPEAN WHEEL – A roulette wheel containing just one zero.

⊛ FURLONG – Track distance is measured in furlongs. One furlong is 220 yards. Eight furlongs is one mile.

⊛ FUTURE BET – A wager selected well in advance.

⊛ GELDING – a castrated colt.

⊛ HANDICAP RACE – In handicap races, weights are allotted according to the rating assigned to the horse by the racetrack handicapper. The weight carried includes the jockey and additional weights in the saddlecloth (in case the jockey isn't heavy enough).

⊛ HANDICAPPER – A person who studies upcoming sporting events and rates them according to how he foresees the outcome.

⊛ HARD HAND – Any blackjack hand that doesn't contain an ace valued at 11 is a hard hand.

⊛ HARD WAY – In craps, this is a roll in which the dice come as a pair for the 4, 6, 8 or 10 (2-2, 3-3, 4-4 or 5-5).

⊛ HEDGING – Placing bets on the opposite side to cut losses or guarantee winning a minimal amount of money.

⊛ HIGH-LOW BET – A roulette bet on either the high numbers (19-36) or the low numbers (1-18). (Pays 1-1).

⊛ HIT – In blackjack, a hit is when the player takes another card.

⊛ HOLE CARD – In blackjack, the hole card is the card that's face down. You don't learn the value of the hole card until after you play your hand.

⊛ HOOK – A half-point added to football and basketball betting lines, making it impossible to push.

⊛ HOUSE EDGE – The percentage of each bet that you make, on average, that the house takes in.

⊛ IN-RUNNING BET – A wager made on an event while the event is in progress.

⊛ INSIDE BET – A roulette wager placed on any individual number on the table, including 0 or 00, or any combination of the numbers.

⊛ INSURANCE – In blackjack, insurance is a side bet that the dealer has a natural. It's only offered when the dealer's up card is an ace. If the dealer has a natural, the insurance bet wins double. If the dealer doesn't have a natural, the insurance bet loses.

⊛ JUICE – The bookmaker's commission; vigorish.

⊛ KENO BOARD – The board displaying winning keno numbers.

⊛ LAY BET – A craps bet in which a wrong bettor bets that a 7 will be rolled before the number.

⊛ LAYING THE POINTS – Betting the favorite.

⊛ LIMIT – The maximum amount a bookmaker will allow you to bet before changing odds and/or the points; or the "cap" on what one person can wager.

⊛ LINE – The listed odds or points on a game.

⊛ LINEMAKER – The person who sets up the original and subsequent betting lines.

⊛ LOW POKER – When playing low poker, the ace is the lowest card and the lowest hand wins. The best possible hand you can have in low poker is – A-2-3-4-5.

⊛ MAIDEN RACE – In racing, a maiden race is one in which none of the participating horses have ever one a race. Horses of both genders are allowed to participate.

⊛ MARE – A female horse, five years old or older.

⊛ MARTINGALE SYSTEM – A well known roulette system in which the player doubles his bets after each loss until he wins.

⊛ MIDDLING – Winning both sides of a single betting proposition. (For example, betting the favored team at -6½ with one bookmaker and then taking the underdog at +7½ with another bookmaker. If the favorite wins by 7 points, you win both bets. With all other outcomes, you push.)

⊛ MINI-BACCARAT – A scaled-down version of baccarat, played with fewer players and dealers; the rules are the same as baccarat.

⊛ NATURAL – In blackjack, a natural is a two-card hand worth 21 points (the best possible score).

⊛ ODDS-ON FAVORITE – A team or athlete so heavily favored that the odds are less than even.

⊛ ODDSMAKER – Linemaker.

⊛ ONE ROLL BET – A craps bet in which the outcome is determined by the next roll of the dice.

⊛ OPENING – In poker, the player who bets first is opening.

⊛ OUTSIDE BET – A roulette bet on red, black, odd, even, high, or low.

● OVER/UNDER – A wager in which you bet on whether the final score of a sporting event will be either higher or lower than a number specified by the oddsmaker.

● PARI-MUTUEL – A French term that translates loosely to "mutual stake." Odds for a pari-mutuel betting system are determined by the bettors. The track takes a fixed percentage of the pot and the rest is divided among the winning bettors.

● PARLAY – A bet in which wagers are made on several events and only pays out if each wager is successful. The advantage is a bigger payout. For example, a two-team parlay typically pays at 13-5 odds, a three-team parlay pays at 5-1 odds, a four-team parlay pays at 8-1 odds, etc.

● PASS LINE – The area on the craps table layout where pass line bets are made.

● PASS LINE BET – A bet in craps that the dice will pass; betting with the dice.

● PAST PERFORMANCE SHEET – A compilation of data on horses based on recent races. The more experienced you get, the more you'll be able to read into a past performance sheet and the more you'll be able to utilize it. Past performance sheets serve as quick references to vital information about horses, such as how they do under certain track conditions and at which distance(s) they are most effective.

● PAYLINE – The line on a slot machine on which the symbols from each reel must line up.

● PAYOUT PERCENTAGE – The percent of each dollar played in a video poker or slot machine that the machine returns to the player.

● PAYOUT TABLE – A posting on the front of a video poker machine telling you what each winning hand pays for the number of credits played.

● PENETRATION – The amount of cards in blackjack that are dealt before the dealer reshuffles all the cards in the shoe. The lower the penetration, the lower the chances of counting cards effectively.

● PICK – A multi-race wager in which the winners of all included races must be selected (e.g. pick three, pick six, pick nine, etc.).

● PICK'EM – A sporting event in which no team is favored.

● POINTSPREAD – The amount of points the bettor must give to wager on a game. If Team 1 is favored and the point spread is 6 1/2, Team 1 must win by seven or more points to cover the pointspread.

● POST POSITION – The position in which a horse starts a race. Post positions are numbered consecutively with No. 1 being closest to the rail.

● POST TIME – The time at which a race starts. Horses line up at the starting gate one or two minutes before post time.

● PROGRESSIVE A slot or video poker game in which the potential jackpot increases with each credit that's played.

● PROPOSITION BET – A wager on a particular aspect of an event, such as how many strikes a pitcher will throw or how many passes a quarterback will complete.

● PURSE – In racing, a purse is the prize money that's distributed to the owners of the winning horses.

● PUSH – A game in which neither side wins and all money is returned to the bettors. For example, if the Packers are favored by 7 and they win by 7, the game is a push.

● QUINELLA – A wager in which the first two finishers must be picked in either order.

● RAIL – The inside edge of a racetrack.

● RAISE/RAISING – In poker, a player raises by matching the previous bet and then betting more, thereby increasing the stake for remaining players.

● RAKE – In poker, a rake is the money that the casino or card room charges for each hand. It's typically a percentage or flat fee that's taken from each pot after each round of betting.

● RED-BLACK BET – A roulette wager on either red or black. (Pays 1-1.)

● RIVER – The final card dealt in a game of stud or Hold'em poker.

● ROUND ROBIN – A parlay bet in which the bettor wagers various combining team wagers. A three-team robin, for example, consists of team 1 vs. team 2, 1 vs. 3, and 2 vs. 3.

● SEVENTH STREET – The fifth and final round of betting in 7 card stud. (Each player has seven cards.)

● SHOE – The box that holds the cards being dealt. Blackjack players who count cards in an effort to determine the likeliness of certain cards being dealt have a much higher success rate when there are fewer decks in the shoe. The amount of decks in the shoe typically varies from one to six.

● SIX-NUMBER BET – An inside combination bet in roulette on six numbers at the same time.

⊛ SIXTH STREET – The fourth round of betting in 7 card stud. (Each player has six cards.)

⊛ SLOW RAIL – a bias in which horses running further away from the rail have an advantage over horses running close to it.

⊛ SNAKE EYES – a craps term for the number 2.

⊛ SOFT HAND – In blackjack, any hand that contains an ace that's valued at 1 is a soft hand.

⊛ SPEED RATING – Horses are assigned speed ratings based on their past performances. The lengths of races and the track conditions are taken into consideration upon the determination of this number. The speed rating relates how fast a horse ran to some standard that allows comparison between different past races.

⊛ SPLIT – In blackjack, players can split hands after two cards are dealt if the two cards are of the same value. Bets are automatically doubled when a player splits.

⊛ SPLIT BET – An inside combination bet in roulette on two numbers at the same time.

⊛ SPORTS BOOK – A facility, online or offline, that accepts wagers on sporting events.

⊛ SPREAD LIMIT GAME – A poker game in which any bet between two limits is allowed at any time.

⊛ STAKES RACE – In racing, stakes races attract the best horses and offer the largest purses. America's Triple Crown races—the Kentucky Derby, the Preakness, and the Belmont Stakes—are examples of stakes races.

⊛ STAND – In blackjack, standing is when you don't take any more cards.

⊛ STANDOFF – A situation in craps in which no decision results from a throw of the dice on certain bets.

⊛ STRUCTURED GAME – Also known as a "fixed-limit" game, a structured game is one in which the first dollar amount is what can be bet or raised in the early rounds, while the second amount is what can be bet or raised in the later rounds.

⊛ STUD POKER – A poker game in which certain cards are dealt face up, while the rest are dealt face down.

⊛ SURRENDER – A rule in blackjack that allows players to bail out of a hand if it looks they're going to lose. Surrendering players give up half their bets for the privilege of not playing out the hand.

⊛ TEASER BET – A bet in which the bettor is allowed to pad the point spread and/or over/under total to improve his chances of winning. The chances of winning are better, but the payouts are much lower.

⊛ THIRD BASE – The nearest seat at a blackjack table to the right of the dealer. The player at third base is the last player to be dealt.

⊛ THIRD STREET – The first round of betting in 7 card stud. (Each player has three cards.)

⊛ TOTE BOARD – A display of the totals bet on the various horses to win, place and show as well as the odds a bettor is likely to receive on win bets. Tote boards are typically updated in one-minute intervals before the start of a the race.

⊛ TRIFECTA – A wager in which the bettor selects the first three finishers of a race in exact order.

⊛ Trio Bet – A combination bet in roulette on three numbers at the same time.

⊛ UNDER – A bet that the combined total points scored by both teams during a game will be under a specified total.

⊛ UNDERDOG – The team or person picked by the odds makers to lose.

⊛ UP CARD – In blackjack, the up card is the card in the dealer's hand that is face up for all players to see before they play their hands.

⊛ VIGORISH – The bookmaker's commission. Also known as "vig" or "juice."

⊛ WIN/PLACE/SHOW – A horse picked to win must finish first. A horse picked to place must finish first or second. A horse picked to show must finish first, second or third.

⊛ WISE GUY – A knowledgeable handicapper or bettor.

⊛ WRONG BETTOR – A Craps bettor whose bets don't pass (against the dice).

APPENDIX VI: A–Z OF INTERNET TERMS

⊛ BANDWIDTH – The amount of data that can be sent through a connection (usually measured in bits per second).

⊛ BIT – The smallest unit of data.

⊛ BPS – Bits per second; the rate at which data is moved.

⊛ CLIENT – Software residing on the machine of the person browsing the Internet. The client is used for obtaining data from server software on a remote computer. A Web browser (such as Internet Explorer) is an example of a client.

⊛ COOKIE – A file sent by a Web server to a Web browser that is saved by the browser and sent back to the server when the browser makes additional requests from the server. Cookies contain information such as registration information and user preferences.

⊛ DOMAIN NAME – A unique name identifying an Internet site.

⊛ DOWNLOAD – The transfer of data from a remote computer to the computer you are using.

⊛ ENCRYPTION – A way of coding information in a file so that if it is intercepted by a third party as it travels over a network it cannot be read. Only persons with the appropriate decoding software can unscramble the message.

⊛ HYPERTEXT – Text on a Web page that contains links to other files (documents, other Web pages, etc.)

⊛ JAVA – a programming language used to build large complex software systems, often used to create animated games. Most Web browsers (and many mobile phones) are equipped with the necessary software to read Java files.

⊛ LOGIN – the account name used to gain access to a computer system.

⊛ MODEM – A hardware device that connects a computer to a phone line. Modems make it possible to download and upload data to and from remote computers

⊛ PORTAL – a Web site that serves as a starting point for surfing the Internet. A gambling portal is a site through which users can access gambling Web sites.

⊛ SEARCH ENGINE – A system used for searching the Internet.

⊛ SERVER – A computer or software that provides service to client software running on other computers. Web sites are housed on servers.

⊛ SPAM – Unsolicited e-mail.

⊛ SPYWARE – Software that's secretly installed on a user's computer and is used to monitor the user's activity without his or her consent. Spyware most often a means of knowing the user's interests and tendencies so that the installer can feed the user targeted advertising.

⊛ UPLOAD – The transfer of data from a the computer you are using to another computer.

⊛ URL – Uniform Resource Locator; a Web address.

ABOUT THE AUTHORS

Mark Balestra is vice president/publishing for River City Group, a St. Charles, MO-based company that provides research, consulting, publications and conferences for the interactive gambling industry, as well as editor of the company's leading electronic trade publication, Interactive Gaming News (www.igamingnews.com). He is also the former editor of RGTOnline.com and has extensive experience as an author, editor and researcher in the field of interactive gambling. His articles have been published in numerous industry- and consumer-related publications and he frequently appears as a speaker at seminars and conferences.

One of the pioneers of online gaming, **Calvin Ayre** founded a software company in 1994 that would eventually become the Bodog.com Entertainment Group of Companies. By 2004, Ayre would be named online gaming's 15th most influential person in the world by *eGaming Magazine*, and Bodog.com is widely considered the most recognizable brand in its space. After earning a Bachelor's Degree in General Sciences and an MBA in Management Finance Ayre, an early adopter of both technology and the Internet, was interested in founding an Internet-based company. In fact, he would sell everything he owned to start the Bodog Group. Originally envisioned as a software company, Ayre quickly switched gears after reading an article about sports betting companies working internationally and utilizing phones for wagering. Ayre believed that the Internet and an independently verifiable event such as sports betting would be a natural fit. The gamble certainly paid off. Bodog.com is now a world leader in online sports betting, casino and poker action. During its growth the Bodog.com Group of Companies has been responsible for many industry innovations in technology, marketing and business models. In recent years, the Bodog.com Entertainment group has expanded its brand into real estate, venture capital, and investment fund management. As founder and CEO of Bodog.com, Mr. Ayre has also published articles on a variety of topics on the online gaming industry in publications such as *eGaming Review*, *iGaming News*, and *Play Savvy*.

Bodog.com Sports Casino Poker located in San Jose, Costa Rica, is federally licensed by the Costa Rican, and UK government. One of the pioneers of online gambling, Bodog.com is the top ranked US facing online gambling brand, recently valued at over US $1 billion, and ranked in the Power 25 online companies.

Adriaan Brink is president of Mahjong Mania (www.mahjongmania.com), a Montreal-based developer of real-money multi-player Internet Mahjong. He was born in Durban, South Africa and completed schooling studying Computer Science at the University of Natal, South Africa. In early 1995, he played a major role in the launching of the word's first legal Internet-based lottery. Operating out of Liechtenstein, InterLotto quickly established its position as a leading e-commerce site in Europe. In 1997, the International Federation of Red Cross and Red Crescent Societies reached agreement to become the major beneficiary and the site was renamed PLUS Lotto (www.pluslotto.com).

As CEO of The International Lottery in Liechtenstein Foundation (www.illf.com), the operator of the lottery, Brink architected the systems and directed the design and development team. He also took care of marketing, sales and charity relationships. In 1998 Brink was a founding director and CTO of Earthport, a UK-based payment services company specializing in direct-from-bank Internet payment mechanisms. In 2001 he formed Zabadoo AG and bought the lottery systems from Earthport. Zabadoo expanded the markets to include new third-party partners marketing branded lotteries.

In 2003 Brink established Genesis Consulting (www.gcon.li) as an independent consultant to lottery and other I-gaming and e-commerce businesses, and moved away from the day-to-day operations of ILLF and Zabadoo. Brink lives in Liechtenstein.

Michael Caselli has been involved in the online gaming industry since 1996 when he completed his Masters work at the University of London (Imperial College of Science, Technology and Medicine) analyzing the viability of gaming on the Internet. Following his academic career, he became a writer and consultant for the online gaming industry, advising strategies for startup online casinos and terrestrial casinos considering their future in online gaming. In 1999 Caselli founded Lyceum Publishing LLC, which produces and publishes the Internet Gaming magazines *Online Casino News* and *The Gambling Daily*. Lyceum Publishing LLC is a daily content provider to online gamblers and the online gaming industry and provides information to approximately 3 million readers monthly. In 2000, Caselli was appointed editor of *Gambling Online Magazine*, the first print magazine dedicated exclusively to Internet gambling. *Gambling Online Magazine* is distributed throughout the USA, Europe, Asia and Australia. The publication is the market leader and the most widely read international online gaming print publication in the world.

In 2003, Caselli took on the role of managing editor for *iGaming Business*, a trade magazine for the online gambling industry. *iGaming Business* is read by terrestrial and online casino professionals and offers operational, management, marketing and legal columns to help them run their interactive gaming businesses more efficiently. Caselli is considered one of the world's leading experts on online gaming and has served as chairman of numerous International forums and conferences that focus on electronic gaming throughout Europe, Asia and America.

Tony Calvin is Betfair's sports betting expert and appears regularly in publications such as the *Racing Post*, the bible for bettors in Britain, where he worked before moving to Betfair in 2001.

Mark Davies was part of the founder management team for Betfair. He has been the company's public face as it has competed with the traditional industry and worked with governments on both sides of the world over the last five years.

Following almost ten years in advertising and marketing, **Phil Fraser** was marketing and commercial head at the launch of the William Hill online casino,

the first major brand to enter the world of online casinos. Since 2001, he has been running i-ludus Consulting, a specialist online bingo consultancy offering strategic planning and marketing services to companies looking to develop online bingo businesses. Clients include land-based companies like William Hill, Littlewoods, Gala Group and Victor Chandler, as well as many of the leading Online Bingo game sites and software providers. Fraser has spoken at many gaming conferences around the world, including EIG, GIF II, EOG and the Virtual Gaming Forum. He is a respected commentator on a wide variety of online gaming issues, with many articles appearing in both on and offline media, as well as BBC radio. He writes a regular online bingo column in *Gambling Online* magazine. He was a contributor to the review of the UK's gaming laws (The Budd Report) and has also worked with the UK government in its planning of the implementation of the online aspects of the recommendations.

Ian Sherrington, born and educated in England, now lives in Montreal, Canada. He has been playing Mahjong since he was at school over 25 years ago and is a devoted fan. He is the president of Mahjong Mania, a software company specializing in online multiplayer Mahjong.

Patrick Smyth is the CEO of Gaming Transactions Inc. and the president of CYOP Systems International Inc. He has been involved in the online skill games and online casino industries since the mid-1990s and has been involved in the launch and marketing of over 100 gaming sites. He is a featured speaker at gaming conferences and is also a contributing author to the International Game Developers Association.

Bradley Vallerius is a writer for Interactive Gaming News, a subscription-based online publication that provides daily news for the remote gambling industry. Over the last two years he has written extensively on interactive gaming topics, including technological developments, market trends, and regulatory issues and legal cases in Europe, North America, Australia and Asia.